PRAISE FOR HOW TO CLOSE SALES APPOINTMENTS

"Focus, drive, attitude, work ethic, integrity, and reading this book will position you above your competition. August provides the framework for competitive differentiation and innovation in the sales process."

—**Jim Regnery**, Vice President, Business Development,
Answerthink

"Mr. Specht hits the target on successful sales strategies and tactics. Businesses are overwhelmed with information in a rapidly changing business environment. Every business has a need for technology, for better processes etc., but no one has the time to sift through the information or to understand various product attributes from various salespeople at various companies. It is the salesperson who takes the time to understand the business, who differentiates why they can help and how they can bring benefit to the decision-maker, and who makes it easy for a business to accept them as their business partner. Mr. Specht has a proven sales track-record, and his common-sense approach defined here will work for anyone."

—**Dan Gay**, Vice President and Chief Marketing Officer,
TOUCHAMERICA

"The key to success is through focus and discipline. This book will steer you toward the achievement of your goals."

—**Tom Fletcher**, MCI Sales Director

"This book contains valuable, hands-on information to avoiding costly and time-consuming mistakes for rookie and seasoned sales veterans alike. I found myself remembering mistakes that I had made early in my sales career and wondering how much further I could have gotten, faster, with a practical guide to real selling, like this book. Written by someone who has *been there and done that*."

—**Justin Matott**, Former MCI Sales Executive, and Random House author of more than ten acclaimed books.

"August has certainly lived what he writes about. As one of the most successful salespeople in one of MCI's top branches, August had the opportunity to practice what he is "preaching." And I can say he had a *very* successful practice."

—**Jim Smithberger**, Sales Vice President of Staff Leasing, Sales Director MCI, Worldcom, Sales Management, AT&T and Notre-Dame Football All American and NFL player

How to Close Sales Appointments

How to Close Sales Appointments

♦

Meet the Right People at the Right Time with the Right Strategy

August J. Specht II

iUniverse, Inc.
New York Lincoln Shanghai

How to Close Sales Appointments
Meet the Right People at the Right Time with the Right Strategy

iUniverse books may be ordered through booksellers or by contacting:

iUniverse
2021 Pine Lake Road, Suite 100
Lincoln, NE 68512
www.iuniverse.com
1-800-Authors (1-800-288-4677)

ISBN-13: 978-0-595-34957-9 (pbk)
ISBN-13: 978-0-595-79668-7 (ebk)
ISBN-10: 0-595-34957-9 (pbk)
ISBN-10: 0-595-79668-0 (ebk)

Printed in the United States of America

For:
My God, who has provided all that I have and am
My father, my hero, who I miss every day
My lovely wife, Tina, for restoration of my hope, love, faith, future, and family
My wonderful son, Augie, for making my life a joy and driving my purpose
For our new baby boy, Roman, for sleeping well, validating our faith, and making our family complete.

Contents

Acknowledgments

This book could be titled *Publishing on a Shoestring Budget.* After my employer was liquidated in the bust of 2001, I found myself with no income, a two-month-old baby, and savings for living, but not for book publishing. My goals and my life were all in a major stall. Several people came forward to help with little to no hope of compensation for their significant contributions of talent, creativity, time, and energy. Carlos (Charlie) Espinosa, who like an answer to a prayer, just happened to be willing and more than able to design the incredible cover that graces this volume. Moral support, mentoring, and guidance were provided frequently over the years by Justin Matott, whose humble yet significant example of success in writing and sales has kept me focused. My lovely wife, Tina, acted as an editor, counselor, and fellow sales leader. My sales mentors: my dad, Joe Carvagno, who is my brother-in-law, Tom Fletcher, Neil Kaiser, Jim Smithberger, Bill Wohlrob, Dan Wood and many others have all set examples for me to follow throughout the many years I have been in the sales profession.

Thanks to all of you.

Preface

The best way to predict your future is to create it.

By reading this book you will be providing yourself with proven techniques that will enable you to succeed in a variety of endeavors. These principles not only apply to making sales appointments, but they also apply to everyday life. They have universal relevance to any situation, whether it's meeting with someone on a sales call, conducting an interview, meeting with an agent or a publisher, or even running for office. The bottom line is to understand people's goals and offer a solution in order to assist in their achievement.

There are many challenges associated with a career in sales, but let's discuss the positives that make it all worthwhile. A sales career is an excellent career for a number of reasons:

1. Money—We can make as much as many lawyers, doctors, and corporate executives. Many of us make over six figures on a consistent basis. We have been able to achieve equivalent incomes in less time without the significant expenses of a post-graduate education. We are way ahead of many high-paying professions.

2. Independence—We have the opportunity to work from home, from the car, from a hotel, from a golf course, from a boat—wherever and whenever we like. Most sales jobs are not the type where you punch a clock or go to the office every day. We have the opportunity to work the schedules and hours we choose, as long as we can still produce. There are many, although not enough, sales executives who have the following management philosophy:

"I don't care how, I care how much."

3. Autonomy—In sales, you are given a territory, and it is your franchise. You will be allowed to run your program however you like, without interference, as long as you show progress and production.

4. Relationships—Through your good word and high standards of integrity, you will meet customers that will trust you. The by-product of that bond is the purchase of your goods and services. The longer-term, more permanent result is that you will be able to meet intelligent, impressive corporate leaders and establish lifelong relationships. Always respect leaders, honor your word, and exceed expectations.

Even in large cities, if you burn your bridges through unethical behavior, you will be out of business in that area across any number of industries. You may have to leave town to start over. Take care of your customers and they will take care of you; if you don't, they won't.

5. Perks—International and domestic travel is often an opportunity. Frequent-flier points afford many of our families free vacations. Expatriate packages still exist for those of you adventurous enough to live overseas. There are incredible opportunities around the world for successful, flexible, salespeople. Free laptops, printers, cell-phones, and planners are often provided with the job. Also, activities can be planned with customers as long as there is a good business reason. Events like golfing, fishing, concerts, and professional sports are all common freebies. We will attend functions like the World Series, the Super Bowl, Daytona 500, the Masters tournament, and many more.

6. Lifestyle—There is the possibility of travel in corporate jets and extensive global touring. I have colleagues who have flown on the Concorde and traveled on the Orient Express. My wife went to Kenya on a safari. There will be trips to Hawaii, and I know someone who won a Mercedes.

These are just a few of the benefits of hard work in a sales career. By reading this book, you are taking the first important step. The rest is up to you: take advantage of my experience, put in the hours, close appointments, make more money, and have fun.

Introduction

I am not discouraged, because every wrong attempt discarded is another step forward.
~Thomas Edison~

Thank you for selecting this book to assist you in achieving your goals. I have written this guide to help you work more effectively, with the ultimate goal of teaching you how to increase your close ratio and to work smarter.

This book is structured into three main parts. The first section comprehensively discusses how to prepare for your appointment setting, covering everything from structuring a territory to evaluating a potential prospect. This is an ideal read if you run your own company, are a sales leader with a territory that needs to be designed from the ground up, or are new to sales. If you have a little more sales experience and have been assigned a territory you may want to skip to the second section, which discusses the actual contact strategies. The third section is a must-read for everyone, for it delves into how to be more effective, what things could halt your progress and how to circumvent them, and how to stay motivated when you are ready to call it quits.

When I started my career in sales almost twenty years ago, there were no similar books to offer assistance or guidance. In my postgraduate naiveté, I believed corporate sales training would provide all the answers. I was ready to learn all the tools of my new trade: whom to call, what to say, and how to close the sale.

The corporate sales training was greatly disappointing, and I returned home and to my new quota dazed and confused. I learned little in Sales School 101 and found myself in the all-too-typical sink-or-swim sales position. After years of sales training, I have determined that most of it is incomplete and a waste of time.

What was missing was the crucial link that salespeople need. All the instructional emphasis on learning how to sell assumed that you had already gotten to the decision maker. Every teacher had you driving the Porsche, but not one of them showed you how to fuel it, turn it on, or even open the door. Training on how to sell is critical, but the subject has been written about time and time again. Anyone that has been in sales for a few years has survived at least five courses, all with different names that teach pretty much the same thing: what to do after you get the appointment.

How many motivational speakers tell you how to get in the door? How many consultants instruct on getting an appointment? Has your manager ever discussed prospecting? The critically important step is getting the appointment. Yet no one has taught this step…until now.

In my career, I have known people that gave me goose bumps when they spoke. These individuals could silence a room with their expertise. There were trainers who could put a classroom of people into hysterics. However, they could not sell. Their lack of sales success had nothing to do with their ability, or knowledge, or work ethic; it was because they couldn't get people to see them.

I have also known salespeople who I thought had no chance of being successful. One interview with them led me to believe that there was no way these people could be successful in sales. They were lacking in important skills required to survive in today's business climate. Yet they proved me wrong, because they had the one skill that was the most important. They could get the appointment and bring in the resources they needed to close the deal.

What does this tell us? Don't bother learning your product. Don't bother polishing your presentation skills. Don't even think about becoming an expert on anything unless you also develop the skill of making appointments by digesting the information in this book.

The organization of this book makes it essential for you to read it through once before applying the lessons. You will find discussions on efficiency, setting goals, and keeping the right frame of mind. You will also find a sales lexicon that will include terms that do not always follow the *Webster's* definition. Throughout the book you will find the words *customer*, *account*, and *prospect*. They are all of a singular meaning and completely interchangeable. The word prospect does not always mean a noncustomer. You can have new prospects and opportunities within existing accounts or with existing customers. This work is a reference tool for you to keep handy for reminders, focus, tips, reassurance, and inspiration.

Good reading and good selling.

PART I
Preparation for the Hunt

The 6 P's:
Prior Preparation Prevents Piss-Poor Performance

1

Territory

Activity does not equal accomplishment.
~Unknown~

The three most important criteria to your sales success are territory, territory, and territory.

Put rookies in a great area and they will be at 400% of quota. Take your best salespeople, put them in a desolate territory, and they will struggle.

The ideal situation would be to avoid this territory roulette and be able to create your own sales territory. However if, like most of us, you have been assigned a territory, it is critical that you do everything you can to understand what type of territory you have, so you can behave accordingly.

In this chapter I will give you the tools to assess whether your territory will allow you to set sales records with ease, or if you will need to drill down very hard to make your numbers. In both cases, you will learn where you should focus your activity in order to be successful. In the latter scenario, this exercise will teach you to determine whether a job or territory change would be a wise idea. Focusing and educating yourself on your territory will allow you to determine your chances and forecast your future.

Before we begin, let me define what a territory is. A territory can be a fixed geography like eight states, or five ZIP codes. It can be an account list and/or a vertical market, or a combination of all three (i.e. the top ten auto manufacturers in Europe).

What is interesting and challenging in maintaining a territory is that each one is unique and has to be structured for the specific industry you are representing. When I sold domestic telecommunications in a five ZIP code area in Florida, I had more opportunity in that market than selling international telecom in an eight-state western territory. The same sales position in Manhattan would be more successful in a few blocks than several Midwestern states. Your territory should be based entirely on what you are selling, instead of the usual random division of geography.

There are two main reference vehicles that I recommend to create and understand your territory. One is Internet based, the other a hard bound book. Both are superior to anything else I have seen in my career. The Internet tool is light years ahead of the book version because of speed, sorting capabilities, and daily information updates. However, the book version (*Contacts Influential*) does offer CD-ROMs and provides basic demographics that will allow you to structure a territory. It also covers all prospects, while Internet sites like Hoover's and most others primarily cover only public or larger private organizations.

We will start with how to handle an existing territory, as odds are that you have to make the best of the territory that has been assigned to you. Then we will show you how to create a territory from scratch.

Before we begin, let me say a few words about focus. As strange as it sounds, prospects reward salespeople for their tenacity with opportunities. I have been complimented numerous times by prospective customers on my persistence in following up with them in a consistent, yet nonharassing manner. When you receive these compliments it is almost as good as closing a deal, since you know that will come.

With a well-planned, well thought-out territory, you will get appointments in one of three ways: wearing them down, having a solution that applies to their goals, or a combination of both. Either way requires selecting a finite number of accounts to concentrate on. You do not want to call everyone in New York City one time. You will be able to sell most of a single skyscraper by contacting each prospect ten times.

The best salespeople focus on a finite number of accounts that are divided by geography, type of business, or account list. They learn everything there is to know about these accounts and outposition their "shotgunning" competition. This focused method results in a higher close ratio, happy, wealthy salespeople, and struggling competitors who cannot hire your people away.

Making the Best of a Bad Situation Using an Internet Based Tool: Hoover's

We will use a real-life example from my most recent territory planning. The goal was to complete a sales plan for an eight-state district. The best way to proceed with the plan was by uncovering all of the top prospects in the area and then focusing efforts on those accounts.

In the past, I used Hoover's Online Web site in a very reactive manner. I would learn of an account through my sales channel, and then do complete research through Hoover's to see where my product and solution would best fit, if at all.

My goal was to change that and find all of the accounts in eight states that did business outside of North America, then use this list to proactively pursue the opportunities. An international plan is the most difficult territory to create. There is not one site on the Internet where you can conduct a search for all international accounts in a given area. Of all of the dozens of sites I researched, Hoover's comes the closest.

I went to their web page HTTP://www.hoovers.com and sorted through the myriad of options of this very robust site. Hoover's offers comprehensive services like business news, leads, newsletters, detailed corporate information, and excellent links to dozens of lists like Best Places to Live and the Forbes 100. Many services are free, while others are subscription-based. The free offer is perfect for researching companies. The primary free information is featured on the Web site through the company capsule. The fee-based services are critical to the design of a territory and researching individuals, and offer significantly more detail than the capsule.

The first step in completing the plan is to use Hoover's advanced search capability. This feature comes at a cost of $199.95 per year or $29.95 per month. The price also includes access to annual reports, full company profiles, executive information (including pay and background), in-depth detailed financials, and competitive comparisons.

To begin the project, go to the home page. Click on the advanced search button at the top of the screen. The advanced search page comes up with a few key options to sort through. You can select your search area by metro area, state, area code, ZIP code, or even country. You are able to further delineate your request by criteria such as company type, number of employees, growth rate, and revenues. Finally, the feature that will be important for many of you is the option to sort by industry or SIC (standard industry classification) code.

If I want to see every account in a state that Hoover's offers, I simply enter California, for example, and press go. The results come back with almost 2000 companies. This is a good example of the random nature in which territories are assigned. Past research in my area (which does not include California) illustrates that between eight states I have roughly 300 hundred total accounts worthy of mention in Hoover's. My two counterparts on the West Coast split up 2300 accounts in California alone.

Back to the grim reality: Arizona is mine, so I enter Arizona and press go, and I get back 129 organizations and companies. Depending on whether or not there is a capsule or a profile, I now select between the two. The capsule gives a short overview of the company and additional information such as: executives, competitors, financials, and my preference: products and operations by segment. This area will show if there are international operations.

The capsule synopsis is usually several paragraphs that provide an overview of the company. It may have already told me that they do international business, but past experience dictates that I also check the products and operations tab for more details.

I click and strike gold. The information not only tells me which countries they do business in, but also that 65 percent of their revenues come from overseas. This is an ideal candidate for my product.

However, Hoover's has more options on this account. I click on the profile option. The profile provides capsule type information with more detail. I also am able to get the complete history of the company and more insight into the goals of the corporation. I also find out that the CEO of the company comes from Finland, speaks four languages, and has established his main goal as greater international expansion.

With this information referenced in front of the customer, I will stand out from my competitors. Home run!

To complete this internationally focused plan, the above procedures are repeated for each account until I have every account in my territory, and can follow the rest of the steps in this book.

Again, international opportunities are cumbersome to research. A more typical scenario would be when I was working in Tampa Bay. I would have conducted a couple of searches for existing territories. One would have been for the Tampa-St. Petersburg area with a minimum of 500 employees. This would return forty-three solid prospects. Another search would be by the diversified services industry (call center companies—big telecom spenders). This would return only one prospect, but it would be a real one with decision making in Tampa Bay, not a subsidiary of a Nebraska call center company with no ability to make decisions in my territory.

Another example would be if I were still selling PBXs like, my first job out of college. I would have done a search of accounts with at least 100 employees and no more than 300, as that was where my product sold best. I would also specify the few ZIP codes I had at that point in time and come up with a list of raw prospects that I would further qualify by cold-calling them. In both of these cases, I had a good territory and there were a significant number of prospects that I could put down on a list and pursue in a strategic fashion as outlined later in this book.

A Book Version: *Contacts Influential*

When I first joined MCI in Tampa Bay, I had two years of experience in that market and knew where business was and was not. Therefore, after I was hired and then assigned a poor territory in very northern Tampa, I was immediately concerned. I drove through my territory with an accelerating ulcer as my fears were confirmed. I went to the only source available back then (pre-Internet), *Contacts Influential*. I scanned the planning section that illustrated the types of companies by size and type per ZIP code. It confirmed my fear. The area was a wasteland of franchises and motels that might be great for someone selling waste management or paper products, but was worthless for me.

In this case, it was critical for me (and for you, if you are in the same boat) to glean the few accounts that fit my target market and slam them hard. The only way that you will have any leverage with a new boss is by proving yourself in your first area. Close the accounts you have and exceed your numbers while lobbying for a new territory. Use these tools to show your manager the disparity in the territories and get a better one as soon as possible.

If you are unsuccessful in making your case, then get another job and negotiate your territory before you accept a position. In my case, I nailed the several accounts that were worthwhile and pestered my boss several times a week for a better area. When one opened up, I was positioned to get it and I rode that territory for four years of big commissions, success, and the beginning of a nine-year gig with MCI. If I had not been given the better area to work, I would have had to quit or eventually get fired, which is what happened to the people who took that first territory after me.

In summary, come away from this part of the plan with a list of the top opportunities within your area. Then follow the rest of the book to meet success in even the worst of territories.

How to Structure an Equitable Territory for All of Your People.

Geographic Territories

There are many ways to go about creating a geographic territory. The most frequently used are by ZIP code and county. If you pursue more of a niche, low-volume market like transportation, you might have a state or even a region to assign. You can reach all of these decisions by using an Internet tool like Hoover's or a hardcover reference tool like *Contacts Influential.*

In each of the above examples, I knew what my target market was. Do you know what yours is? Do you know if your software sells best to mining or finance companies? Do you know if in companies over ten employees your payroll service is not competitive? Do you know that your coffee service is a homerun in white-collar environments, but too pricey in blue-collar environments? If not, you will need to learn fast and lose some deals to find where it fits and where it does not. When you do lose or win a deal, ask the prospect what factors contributed to their decision. If it was just your charm and you can sell igloos to Eskimos, then don't worry about territory. If you are mortal like the rest of us, and you find that your product fits a niche that your competitor's products do not, create a territory based upon those criteria, and then exploit it throughout your jurisdiction.

This learning curve does not only apply to where your product and pricing fits, but also to where you feel most confident. We all feel more comfortable in certain types of accounts. I had a friend that could sell every florist and bowling alley and made a ton of money in the process, but once he got into larger accounts he floundered. You will find your comfort zone where you are most effective by being in front of as many customers as possible.

It is essential that you know where your product fits best. Otherwise, you will be the essence of inefficiency, spending months of energy on prospects that you could never win.

To make this determination, you have several options. One is to check internally with your company. Many companies know where the sweet spot for the service is. Another way is to do your own competitive research. Gather intelligence on your competitors and compare pricing and capabilities to see where you have an edge. Once that is accomplished, then you can proceed to planning your territory.

Hoover's Online—From the earlier section you know how to use the tools. Now apply the same techniques to design equitable areas for yourself or your sales force. Keep in mind proximity to the office, people's homes, what area they network in, and where they grew up. It doesn't make sense to take a person out of an area where he or she well meshed. Again, no Web site covers all of the businesses in a specific area. If you are looking beyond the Fortune 1000, then *Contacts Influential* is the more thorough resource to utilize.

Contacts Influential—Businesses are first organized by county or section of a state, then listed alphabetically, by ZIP code, and by SIC code (vertical market). The area of interest specific to creating territories is the Market Planning section, which sorts companies by number of employees in two ways: ZIP codes and vertical markets (SICs).

Looking at the different ZIP codes, you will see drastic differences from one to the next. The lowest numbers will be your primarily residential areas. The highest numbers may be one of two things: an excellent business area, or a large retail area like a mall or a strip with fast food franchises. Your personal knowledge of the area and a drive through will help complete the picture as to whether these retail areas should be added to your formula, or whether a percentage taken out, if small retail establishments are not your target.

A telephone system salesperson would wither and die in the retail area, but my brother-in-law, a paper products salesperson, would be in Heaven. Taking retail into consideration, you should add all the businesses together between all the ZIP codes listed in the book. Once you get that number, begin to determine headcount.

Use an example of 30,000 opportunities and split it up for allocation between salespeople. For a telecommunications salesperson reliant on a medium-sized business, the first thing you do is throw out the forty people and below group, narrowing down the 30,000 businesses dramatically because it is the largest group in any business community. Now the number is down to 10,000; divide it by how many salespeople you want in that territory.

To further delineate headcount there are two important questions to the sales manager and business owner.

Question one: Do you want to have a lot of sales reps with a minority making their numbers, but your products being pitched in most of the deals in town?

My answer is that you may get a lot of deals short term but your attrition rate in salespeople will be too high.

Question two: Do you want to have just a few salespeople making a lot of money, but missing some opportunities?

I recommend the latter strategy of fewer successful salespeople. They will stay with your company and pick and close the most profitable deals

The former strategy will result in your unhappy reps quitting and taking deals with them to the competition. To avoid this, a good technique is starting with a small number of salespeople. If they are very successful, promote them, and add a couple more.

Therefore, divide the 10,000 accounts by ZIP codes between several reps and turn them loose.

Enforce the territory segmentation, or your strategy will fail. Someone will always have a cousin, or in-law, that is influential in someone else's territory. Try and have the reps settle disputes between themselves, but if it becomes chronic it will dilute your intent of effective territory coverage. Once you have established the territories, they have to be the law; be careful with exceptions, as the salesperson's favorite saying is:

"Don't ask permission, beg forgiveness."

I cannot stress enough the importance of geographic territories for—at minimum—your entry-level salespeople. There is no good reason to have five of your reps driving an hour to the same territory and leaving the office park across the street uncovered. By having a geographic territory for each of your salespeople, you will feel confident that most of the opportunities are covered, and that the salespeople are not just cherry picking the high-attention, low-profit accounts that all the competition read about in the morning paper.

If you are working a geographic area versus an account list, I recommend that you have an informal targeted account list (minimally) that you can focus on within the geography.

Account Lists

Account lists normally cross geographical areas, and are often set up primarily based upon revenue potential. The purpose of account lists is to have fewer prospects that are of a larger nature, so you will focus your attention on a more finite area.

I have seen this entire concept destroyed by people having an account list of hundreds that they cannot effectively work. If you find yourself in this position, create your own sub-list of the best accounts and discard the rest.

You cannot shotgun a territory and be successful. You will end up with a five percent closing ratio and a heart condition.

It depends on the industry, but for the most part a salesperson should not work with more than fifty prospects. Certainly they will clamor for more, but the time to sell and maintain just a percentage of these will make even fifty difficult to manage.

The number of accounts depends on the nature of the job. Is your responsibility and account list strictly acquisition prospects that do no business at all with your company? Or is your position strictly farming? Or is it a combination of both? The more current customers you have, the smaller the account list. The fewer current customers, the larger the list.

The constant pressure applied on a finite number of accounts will result in more sales.

Creating an account list is very simple as long as you know your focus. For example, assume you are selling temporary employment services and there are a group of rookies in geographies selling to companies of fifty employees or fewer. To focus on the larger, more complex deals with more opportunity and a longer sales cycle time, you hire a few top gun salespeople. Go to one of the resources and conduct a search for employers with fifty people or more within your jurisdiction. If you are in Omaha, you may find that one person can adequately cover the forty or so different companies. If you are in downtown Chicago, you have an entirely different headcount requirement.

Vertical Markets

Vertical marketing is a brilliant concept that will work in some environments and fail in others. In deciding whether or not to introduce this concept into your sales force, please consider my thoughts. On the positive side, it is an excellent way to focus individuals in a specific industry (i.e. banking or transportation). A salesperson can become an expert in an industry, then take that expertise and sell the entire sector regardless of geography. I have often been able to leverage my expertise in a particular vertical like healthcare and retail into making appointments with other companies in that sector. It is very easy to get an appointment with a decision maker when that individual hears in your pitch that your solutions have benefited his top competitors. Your salespeople end up as experts in these areas, with solid ongoing revenue results.

However, there are potential negatives. One is that if you have metro sales teams versus a national team, the particular geography may not have a very strong vertical segmentation. There are certain markets, like Tampa or Salt Lake City, that are very generalized, and a vertical specialist may lack enough opportunity to be successful. The other possibility is the exact opposite: that in a town like Los Angeles, you give one sales person entertainment as a vertical, and that account manager has a significant advantage over his peers. You can end up with a huge morale issue and high attrition in the remainder of your sales force.

Therefore, in a national setting or larger metropolitan market, vertical geographies would be a strong consideration, but in those smaller cities you could have huge issues.

Another negative to verticals is that you can create salespeople whose experience is so specialized in one specific sector that they lack knowledge in other industries. Another consideration is the strength of your product in specific verticals. Can you truly, effectively compete in all verticals? Don't always trust marketing on this one, for it could lose you some top salespeople. I had a colleague in Florida who was assigned to hospitality when our hospitality offering was garbage. He starved, and those of us in geographic territories made a fortune.

The benefits of vertical marketing are tremendous in those markets that will support it. There are certain product sets and/or business segments that require this type of attention. However, in most cases, I believe the negative effects on a salesperson's long-term skills are not worth it. Concentrate on physical territories or diverse account lists instead, and the salespeople will have the education and skills of generalists and good business people. This will make them more able to move up to management and assist their reps in every market, and could also facilitate better teamwork.

Nonetheless, vertical markets are very popular, so we will proceed. Consider the case of a company that wants to target top banks within a state. Go to Hoover's and enter the state and the industry classification for banks. If your product sells best in the larger banks, exclude banks under 200 employees and do the search. If you only get a few results, reconsider the approach. Make it a regional position and search several states using the same criteria. If that is still ineffective, consider combining banking with another industry such as financial services or insurance.

2

Research

Some men go through a forest and see no firewood.
~English Proverb~

Why research? In order to sell these accounts you must know them better than your own company. Know their number of employees, locations, annual revenues, goals, competition, and challenges. Learn it all.

Research allows you the opportunity to differentiate yourself from the competition. Your customers need to have a business reason to see you, something that benefits them. You determine that angle and gain access to the account via research. Once the research is completed, you can go after the account knowing what keeps your customer awake at night, and show them a solution. Not only will you have a customer, but also probably a friend, and on occasion a job offer.

Not only do you need to intimately know potential customers, but also your territory. This territory research process should have already taken place from a very high level when creating your territory. However, the deep, detailed investigation of your target area begins now.

There are multiple ways to research your territory. Do not rely on any single source. Consult various methods to have a well-rounded approach to finding your accounts.

Cold-Calling/Knocking on Doors

I've got to prospect
I hate prospecting
I'm allowed to hate prospecting
I've still got to prospect

The first method is the most basic, time consuming, and thorough—cold-call your territory. Cold-calling is not telemarketing, but is defined as physically going through your territory and to prospects' facilities. This is also referred to as knocking on doors. The best way to get an inside look is to visit their headquarters. I spent the first year and a half of my sales career strictly working the phone, "Dialing for dollars," going for the quantity in lieu of the quality. I had a manager that came from copier sales, and he pushed me into knocking on doors.

I was able to get a visual perspective on companies I had been pursuing over the phone. Many of these prospects were not worth my while, and only looked good on paper via flawed sources. Initially, it was my perception that driving through a territory is inefficient and the phone would cover more ground. After that day my philosophy changed, as it was clear that the phone technique had cost me. The cold call is the absolute best test to qualify prospects.

For example, during that first day, I came across an account that I had been telemarketing. Its name was Hav-A-Tampa Cigars, and unlike many of the others, I was pleased to see that this account fell right into my target profile. As I admired the full parking lot, which always indicates a good prospect, I found a good spot right in the front. I parked and began to walk towards the main entrance, when I was interrupted by a loud voice saying that I would not make a good impression by parking in his spot.

I turned around to see a man in a big, black executive sedan. I apologized profusely and moved my car. We walked in together, and he turned out to be the executive vice-president of the company. He was about three or four layers above the individual that I had been calling. Like many executives, he was good-natured. I gave him the pitch and he gave me his card, a referral to another high-level individual, and permission to use his name when calling.

On another day of cold-calling, I came across a very large account. I had just gone in, and I had my head handed to me by the desk sergeant (receptionist). I was standing in front of the office entrance recovering from the experience when an executive car pulled up to the spot right in front of me. I took notice of the name on the concrete marker and it matched the name of the company's owner. I slammed him with a sales pitch before he could even close the car door.

Besides exposure to executives that you would never otherwise bump into, you learn a lot about the organization by visiting the site. The parking lot tells you how many employees they have. It also shows if they are experiencing rapid growth, as the parking lot will be overflowing into neighboring lots.

Good salespeople get excited when they see overcrowded parking lots. This indicates a company with a lot of growth activity, which means there is often need of your solutions.

The parking lot can also tell you what the company does. In the long-distance business, the absolute most arousing moment of cold-calling comes when you see people standing around outside smoking. This is the sign of a call center, which means high telecommunications spending and large commission checks.

Look at the types of cars. If they are beat-up, dingy autos, then maybe it is a sweatshop operation with poor credit, or a company that has poor business ethics and does not pay well. Are there any executive parking spaces, and what types of cars are there?

The grounds can also tell you about the nature of the company. A well-kept property equals a well-run outfit, while the poorly maintained property often means a poorly run operation. Is the company sign outside damaged?

Look for details like graffiti or litter. For example, there was a prospect with a dead-end street sign on the private road entrance to the employee parking lot. After the company failed to meet payroll, an employee painted the sign to read, DEAD END JOB.

Enter the foyer and take note of the company decor. The entrance to the facility is where the company wants to make its first impression. A drab entrance is a clue to your prospect's credit worthiness and whether you should even pursue this account.

If you get a chance, take a look around the lobby. Is there a mission statement? Some companies have mission statements that say they will always see salespeople to keep abreast of discovering new technologies and more efficient ways of doing business. Others have discussed good relationships with their vendors in a partnering setup. These are important philosophies that you need to take advantage of in your approach.

Are there awards and recognition? Is the employee of the month featured? Is there a photo album showing group activities? The fact that these types of employee-oriented items are there, or are missing, speaks volumes about the management, morale, and how you may be treated.

How many people do they have at the front desk? If you see two working switchboards, this company is having trouble dealing with their growth. It also means that with having two people to answer the phone, they have extra cash. Is the receptionist too busy to talk to you because the phone is constantly ringing? This is inefficient and cheap. Are you greeted with an empty cube or a buzzer? They can't afford a receptionist, and are cutting costs and price conscious.

Make sure that you sign or pretend to sign the guest register to see if any of your competitors have visited. If so, whom are they visiting, and what was the duration of their stay? In case your competition also reads the register, you may want to forget to put down your company name and/or whom you are seeing.

When the receptionist does talk to you, make sure you have your pitch down. The average salesperson goes in and asks who makes the decisions for their product. Even though the average employment time for a receptionist is under six months, they usually know not to give out names to salespeople. They are also prepared for you from the minute you walk in the door, because you look like the twentieth salesperson that they have dealt with that day.

The days of seeing a person on the fly without an appointment are over, so surprise the desk sergeant by not being aggressive. Always use an approach that disarms the typical rejections.

The seminar method is very effective: "Hi, my name is August Specht, my company wants to invite a representative of your company to a seminar. The problem is that I do not have an address or a contact person." At this point they will quickly give you an address, during which time you can ask if they have someone like a CFO or a vice president of finance, or whoever it is you want to target. Your explanation would be that the seminar is geared towards these types of people. Don't allow them to pigeonhole you into the wrong place. If they ask if your visit is about a specific product, dodge and repeat the seminar invitation. Emphasize a title, instead of a responsibility, and you will avoid interpretations of what you need. This is because the receptionist might claim the responsibility, but they can never claim the title.

This technique will also work over the phone, but without all of the visual benefits. This method works at least 90 percent of the time. The other ten percent, you can phone and ask for human resources. Once you get past there, say that you were trying to reach the CFO's office, but your call was misdirected, and what was that person's name again? If that still does not work, then pretend to be a delivery company and have a delivery for the CEO. A business organization is another good example, say that you want to invite the CEO to chair a small business meeting but you don't have the name or proper spelling. There are plenty of ways to get around the front desk, just be creative and take some risks. This is not a lapse of ethics, just a name for a letter.

While you are talking to the receptionist, take advantage of the fact that you are meeting the individual with whom you will be speaking more than your desired contact. Find out his or her name and write it down so that when you call for your contact, you can begin to cultivate a relationship. This seeming opponent can also be a coach and advocate to your efforts. They can tell you when your competition is in, when your contact is available, and the best times to reach them. When they do help you, make sure that you reward them. Some memento like an umbrella, some flowers, candy, or golf balls will go a long way. As a result of this relationship, they may even put pressure on your contact to see you.

When you have finished talking to your new friend, make sure you go to the bathroom. No kidding. You may get a look into the main office area and most importantly more information. These days, many companies are putting extension listings in public places like visitors' rest rooms and in the reception area. The extension listing is a jewel of information and is easy to get. On one sheet of paper, you will have all the names, titles, extensions, pagers, e-mail addresses, and direct numbers for the company. An extension listing can be one of your most valuable tools. Take down some notes and move on to the next prospect.

Reading

While cold-calling is my preferred method to get a good firsthand view of the company, the best way to get inside information is by reading everything available about the company. The annual report is the best way to find out about the company's objectives, strategic initiatives, and roadblocks, as well as compensation and personal biographies on the executives that include college, age, and previous employers. This is vital information as you target whom to pursue and sell your product/service to.

The annual report is also a gold mine of information for you to use in a letter to your contact. Consider the effect of quoting the CEO from the letter to the shareholders section while explaining how your product will assist the company in attaining the CEO's goal. Many times I have read through an annual report and highlighted whole paragraphs where the CEO discusses a major initiative that my product would fit perfectly. Take those quotes and send them back to the CEO. Explain how your product will benefit their company.

I have also seen annual reports where they include quotes from various heads of departments on their specific objectives. Use these to your advantage.

Another good source of information is the prospectus that is sent out to potential investors. It provides much of the same information as the annual report, and also provides insight into their industry, challenges, and who is getting what shares of the stock. The prospectus is designed to give the investor insight into all of the variables associated with investing in the company. You will get an excellent read into their hurdles. Your responsibility will be to show how your offer can help overcome those challenges.

Throughout this book, I will often discuss assisting customers by overcoming their challenges with your products. There can be no better way to sell than by partnering with them in accomplishing their goals. There are many challenges that you can assist a prospect with. They include cost cutting, improving their customer service, efficiencies, profitability, or even sales. Get out of the box of what you are selling and think of creative ways to assist your customers. Your competition won't.

Many of your customers will be private companies that don't put out an annual report or prospectus. You will have to be creative on gaining information on the majority of private companies. Hoover's Web Site will often be the solution, and when they don't deliver, CorporateInformation.com is an excellent alternative. If you fail with those two, a general search on Google or Yahoo will usually generate some information. It is hard to believe, but not every company has a Web page; and, not all that do provide the type of information you need.

In addition, the library is a great place to do research. Investigate periodicals to see if there has been any mention of the company in any of the national or local media.

Make sure you visit the company and see if they have an internal newsletter lying around the lobby. I was once able to get detailed information about the decision maker this way, and quote him during our initial phone conversation. I closed the appointment and the deal.

Read every newspaper business section in that geography. I used to get the local business journal, two local business magazines, and had an Internet site send me e-mails whenever a company I was pursuing was mentioned in an article. It takes a lot of my time, but you must know everything that is happening in your backyard or you are losing money.

The local papers have a wealth of information that you cannot afford to miss. Remember that your competition is reading them, too. When you read these business-oriented publications, you will be impressed by the fact that they know so much of what is going on in your territory. These writers have sources, and they need more of them, so become one of their resources. Take the writer out to lunch and swap information before the story hits the press. Reporters can give valuable leads to you weeks before your competition. Tailor the information you provide to them to benefit noncompetitors.

Other sources include international trade directories, Chamber of Commerce publications, and the company's quarterly/monthly internal reports. Always try the Internet first, and the sites and sources listed in the appendix of this book.

Another way to gain information would be an old-fashioned way called spying, or to be more politically correct—networking. Call noncompetitive companies in your city that would know about activities in your account. Office supplies, copiers, telephone systems, commercial real estate, movers, postage stamp sellers, advertising, office furniture, caterers, temp office suppliers, long distance, alarm systems, coffee companies, and more, all have salespeople who are trying to get in to your accounts and sell products and services.

When you contact the company, ask for a sales manager. Explain your call, and tell them that you want their best rep to work with. In good faith, and to sell the manager, proactively provide a couple of good leads.

Meet the reps over lunch, initially on you, and cultivate a relationship. Get four of these people and create a regular weekly or monthly meeting where you exchange leads, referrals, sales practices, and resumes. Many of these partners are already selling to your accounts, and can help get you in the door in exchange for equal treatment.

It is easy to support lead sources. Every time you are talking or meeting with a prospect, keep your eyes and ears open. The visitor register at the front desk will show if any of your network's competitors have visited. The prospect will often complain about proposals they are considering for other services. Be cognizant of company logos on proposals sitting in plain view in their office. Become a good lead source and quota ceases to be a challenge.

In establishing a network, you will find people that are friends with the person whom you can never reach. You will learn where the decision maker brings his kids to play soccer, where he likes to eat and play golf. This is an example of working smart instead of just hard. This method will allow you to play golf on Fridays and be at 300% of your plan instead of being at 100% and working eighty-hour weeks.

What to Look For

While you research, be on the lookout for red flags. One example is impending events, which are outlined below. Other criteria to look for include the following:

Financial difficulties—Companies are usually more open to new ideas when they are struggling.

High attrition rate—With frequent employee turnover lies great opportunity for solutions geared towards alleviation of this problem.

High operating costs—The account may be heading towards financial difficulty if they do not contain their costs. If you have a service that will assist in reducing overhead, this is what to look for in their financial information listed in their annual report.

Executive backgrounds—Where did these people go to college, where did they grow up, what are their hobbies, where do they live? Find an area of commonality and exploit it in your pursuit of an appointment.

Impending Events

Customers often need a catalyst to review changes in established vendor relationships. While reading, cold-calling, and meeting with your network, keep your eyes open for the impending event. An impending event is something that will force the customer to focus their priorities on that activity. Examples of impending events are relocations, expansions, acquisitions, layoffs, initial public offerings (IPOs), reorganizations, and new management.

Every one of these developments changes the way the company does business. For instance, new management will bring in new strategies and change that could assist you in gaining entry to the account. Relocation presents an opportunity for a customer to revamp everything from toilets to telephones, and is an excellent entry for you. Layoffs and reorganizations mean that the company is changing their size, their structure, and the way they do business. They will need technology and infrastructure from sales folks to help implement the change.

Therefore, be on the lookout for the blessed impending event. Be warned that these are often highly prospected events, and you will be in for a fight. It is better to have a relationship with these companies in advance so when the announcement is made of this event, you have a couple of months lead on the fusillade of competitors. Chapter 7 will help you develop this relationship and position you ahead of the pack.

Qualifying

Another goal of research is qualifying. If you can't qualify, you can have a great-looking forecast and still miss your numbers month in, month out. Qualifying is the diligent exercise of determining whether or not the account that you are pursuing is viable, and whether or not you are working with the proper person.

Qualifying is learning when a prospect is "glad-handing" you instead of being sincere. The glad-handers are always glad to shake your hands, always glad to see you, always glad to hear from you, always glad to take your ideas, and always glad to never buy anything from you.

Learning who these people are in advance will make it very liberating to walk away from the bad accounts and focus on the real opportunities. To determine the real versus fake prospects, you must research your accounts thoroughly via credit checks and your network of fellow vendors to establish if these organizations pay their bills, regularly waste salespeople's time, or if they are just straight-out unethical. Do your research, and you will be able to avoid wasting a year of time and perennially forecasting an account that will never close. I have been tempted to discuss a particular account even with a competitor to save time and trouble.

Tracking Activity

Where do you store the results of your research? Don't trust your memory, it is best used for more important tasks. The old way of gathering information was with the 3x5-inch note card. All of the company and contact information went on the card with the history of each call attempt. This card went into a metal box filed in chronological order according to your next follow-up date.

Technology has made this technique outdated. However, you still have to take a notebook when you visit an account and take copious notes of what you see and hear. Now, the method is the computer and software programs that allow you to scan business cards. Use a laptop or PC with activity-tracking software like ACT! or Telemagic for the specific purpose of tracking prospects. These programs are also where all of your research notes should be entered.

You can also customize fields in the software to accommodate any information that you are trying to assemble, whether it is strategies, executives' birthdays, children's names, best time to call, and so on. Harvey McKay's books, *Swim with the Sharks* and the *McKay 66,* outline the type of information that you should know about your contacts in order to sell them and maintain them for years to come.

For those of you that prefer a hard copy that is always by your side, a planner will work instead. FranklinCovey makes the best, most comprehensive planner with flexibility built in. It can be a planner, a tickler file, a project folder, an address book, a goal planner, and more, all built into one package, and the batteries never run out.

3

Positioning

What the fool does in the end, the wise man does in the beginning.
~Proverb~

Positioning is the process of deciding what title the person in a company you should meet with to best advance your efforts holds. This is accomplished by researching individuals to understand where your solution fits.

Using the information in the last chapter, you discovered your main prospects. Now, we will take this information a step further to ensure success. We will research the individuals that work for the company and tie their responsibilities, goals, objectives, and their ability to make buying decisions with your company's offerings to make a match.

Within the selected number of accounts you are focusing on, you need to determine who the decision maker is for your product. When approaching an account for the first time, go slowly and think it through. Whom do you want to call? Do not call just anybody. This can lead to months of frustration with no results. Getting an appointment is not as important as getting one with the right person. A meeting with the wrong person can be disastrous for your opportunity. Aim high and aim well.

Although earlier I suggested getting names from the receptionist on a cold call, do not call these people without first checking with your lead sources for a referral, verification of responsibility, insights into personality, vendor relationships, and biases. The goal is to increase your close ratio by avoiding people who cannot do anything but say no.

Customize your strategy for your market strength. For example, if you are an IBM-type company that sells on value and solutions instead of on price, position at the right level (i.e., chief executive officer [CEO] or chief information officer [CIO]). If you are a discount company selling on price, go for the chief financial officer, where cost and savings are the main focus.

Be careful how you make your bed because you are going to have to lie in it. The decision you make now will determine with whom you will be living with for the next year or more. Once you know which functional area your solution fits best, go after that title throughout your territory.

Many sales managers and trainers will tell you to go straight to the top. Have something to present at that level. The message seems to stop at getting to the top. This book will gain you an audience, but the opportunity will be squandered if you do not speak to their level. If you get there, give them a compelling reason to see you again. If you position yourself as a vendor and not a partner, you will be forced down to a lower level.

The bottom line is this: Don't get in at the wrong level, because you are wasting your time. The nation is full of office managers ready to waste your time and ruin your career by telling you that they make the decisions, which can take place in the next two weeks. This is bull. They initiated the proposal because they don't like their copier or coffee service or phone system, and want to push their boss to change it. But executives don't want to waste time and money, and will not buy anything unless you can give them a compelling reason. The office manager cannot and will not effectively deliver your message, and will block your attempts.

If the annual report has a letter from the CEO discussing a new initiative that your product fits, run—don't walk—to the computer and put together a letter explaining how your product will help the CEO achieve his goals. Drop it off and follow up. This is positioning.

Let the CEO call the meeting and he or she will invite subordinates. There will be ruffled feathers, but you did not go over their heads since there was no previous relationship. These are easy fences to mend with golf or lunches. Make them look good with your product, and all will be forgiven.

I cannot emphasize enough the need to have an account plan, however informal, before setting the appointment. When you make the appointment, congratulate and even reward yourself, but remember one of my favorite quotes:

"Activity does not equal accomplishment."

Do not set activity goals for yourself, set production goals.

An associate started a new job and had no background in pursuing new business via prospecting. We discussed the contents of this book over lunch and he asked me a question pertinent to targeting. He did not know whom to call to effectively position his product. We discussed the background of his telecom company. Initially, we concluded it would be best to pursue someone in the IT group. After further evaluation, we determined that the top benefit of his product was based upon financial savings to the customer. This product positioned in the technological area would be met with a yawn, but presented to the CFO and purchasing area would be welcomed. Apply considerable thought to who benefits the most from your product and pursue those individuals.

Another example was meeting one of my competitors at a training program and comparing war stories on various accounts. It was amazing to hear him discuss the same company names being offered similar products by both of us. One of the reasons I always won was because of whom I was talking to. He was approaching the purchasing department with a value-added solution, which they had no interest in; I was approaching the strategy and IT departments in the same vein.

Target the right person. Find out who they are through your lead sources and research, then follow the next chapter.

Lateral Positioning

Depending on your product set there is usually more than one department to position yourself within an organization. One of my employers had products that were broad enough in scope to apply to a variety of departmental areas such as human resources, marketing, finance, and technology.

We pursued lateral positioning when our competition had the business locked in at one level or when we had hit a wall with a certain individual. Lateral positioning is the alternative to simply moving on to the next account due to an obstacle.

In order to penetrate the account and develop relationships, target another functional group with a product that your competition either does not have or has not tried to sell. By being in more places than the opponent, you will outposition them. The goal is to erode your competitor's market share in diverse areas within the account, or to create market share with totally new services.

With this strategy successfully deployed, when the customer goes to bid for the whole enchilada, we would be a known and proven entity, with a proven reputation of being more thorough than our competition. When the impending event comes along, you are way ahead of the pack and positioned to win not on price, but on value and performance.

Common Titles

The chief executive officer (CEO) is the title you will hear the most often and the one person with whom you will likely never meet. Everyone with whom you will work rolls up to this individual, and all are subject to the CEO's whims, strategies, goals and vision. Having a meeting with this person, albeit great, is not as likely as having access to his or her goals and strategies, and shaping your entire sales plan around them. Take their words to the rest of the organization, sing their song, and you will be well received. All of the employees' careers are tied to meeting the CEO's expectations.

The president is the next level down from the CEO and the individual that handles the day-to-day operations of the entire company. This position is responsible for implementing the visions of the CEO and making it all happen. Services that help the company achieve one of the stated goals should be positioned at this level.

The chief financial officer (CFO), as stated by the title, is dedicated to the organization's finances and is responsible for budgeting, negotiating contracts, driving expenses down, and contributing towards increasing the earning per share.

Anyone who has the misfortune of reporting to this individual will find that their boss will review their strategies for costs instead of value. The term CFO can be a curse to value-oriented salespeople intent on selling profitable services. If you find yourself with this person, double-check your math, and spend time learning the company's financial goals and obligations.

The more profitable the organization is, the less apt they are to beat you up for the best price. If the company is in financial bad shape, you will get in the door quickly, but so will every one of your competitors. Your gratification will end at the appointment. It will be a financial bloodbath, and the lowest bid will probably win.

The chief information officer is the newest title in the executive staff, and in some instances rolls up to the CFO. Due to the significant impact that technology has on a company, this has—for the most part—changed so that the CIO now reports directly to the CEO, and is among the key visionaries. CIOs are in the difficult position of having to be experts in bleeding edge technology and evaluating which strategy is in the best in which to invest. They value salespeople who act as a resource in education on technology and form partnerships to assist in accomplishing their objectives.

For years I worked with a CIO who valued my input because I brought in another vendor who solved a major problem, which made him look good with his boss. The CIO dreads the possibility of the CEO asking about technology with which he or she is unfamiliar. As a fellow technologist, act as a consultant that brings in new ideas and concepts. Along with the marketing people, these folks are the most pro-partner that there is.

The vice-president of human resources is responsible for employee relations, benefits, hiring, firing, sometimes training, payroll services, and telecommunications. This position can be the dumping-ground for responsibilities that may not fit under other job titles. Any product that assists in providing benefits and improving employee morale will be well received by this group.

The vice-president of marketing is responsible for marketing the company's products. If you can bring products to bear that will assist in selling or increasing their product exposure, you will make a good friend and have a coach to push your efforts throughout the company.

The vice-president of purchasing is one of the titles that I have always tried to avoid. These individuals are focused on cost only. Don't go here unless you have a dirt-cheap product.

Other titles to avoid at all costs are office manager, administrative assistant, consultant, analyst, and accounts payable. These people usually have no authority; they will waste your time and keep you from the true decision makers.

Farming Positioning Techniques

Many of us are given a territory that is not of our choosing, but we also get existing customers and associated contacts. These contacts range in responsibility from the tool belt guy, to office manager, to the occasional executive. Whatever the case, we begin our relationship with that organization with someone with whom we may not prefer to work. In fact, we may desperately want to get away from this individual, but are not sure how to do it without losing what business we already have. We are positioned at this level due to the errors of the previous account managers or an internal customer organization issue. Regardless of why, we have to play the cards we are dealt as if the game is poker, not go fish.

Many of our customers are power-hungry and do not want to give up any of their authority. The less authority they have, the less reason for their position. Therefore, the more power someone has, the bigger his or her empire, and the greater perceived job security. To work throughout an organization requires that you must get around this containing individual.

Why? What is the purpose and benefit of going elsewhere in a company when you already have the business? Why jeopardize the entire business relationship just to meet other players?

The answers lie in other questions. How often do you change positions in your career? When you do, don't you bring new ideas and plans? What happens when your contact leaves and someone else is hired whose cousin works for the competition? What happens if your competition follows the advice in this book and starts winning business in other areas that you haven't been able to address? The answers to these questions should show you just how vulnerable you are. The bottom line is that you cannot be single-threaded into your account if you want to retain and grow the business. When your contact does make this inevitable career change, you need to have a lobby of individuals to fight on your behalf when the new person comes in with their own ideas. One of these individuals might be promoted to become your main point of contact. The goal is to create a grassroots support group to keep the business safe.

To create this lobby, you will need to meet other areas and establish credibility. Outlined in the differentiation chapter are techniques and reasons for meeting with other areas like marketing, human resources, finance, purchasing, and so on.

But the question remains: Will your contact allow you to meet with other people, or will they perceive it as a threat to their power?

There are two main techniques in maneuvering through an organization. One is overt and the other is covert. Which method you choose will be determined by the quality of your relationship with the customer.

If the relationship is solid and the customer an adult, you may be able to get their support to meet other functional areas of the company.

This parallel positioning can be part of normal business functions. For example, the one thing all salespeople's products have in common is that they will invoice. Therefore, ensure that you meet and establish relationships at the accounting level. If there are billing issues, it is a great opportunity to demonstrate your value beyond just selling the account. Get the problem fixed, and you will have a supporter.

Most likely your service also includes contracts and legal documents. Make your contractual dealings nonconfrontational and build another alliance.

Whether your contact is in finance or not, you will probably have an opportunity to meet the CFO or controller to review your pricing and math, and begin a relationship there as well.

Under the premise of a good relationship, always inform and ask permission of your main point of contact. Outside of those above-mentioned routine business relationships, you will have to sell your contact on why he should ask his peer or superior to spend time seeing you. Make it a compelling pitch that has benefits for their reputation and career path. If you have an idea that will help the company's marketing department, your contact in finance will get team player kudos.

From a covert perspective, things get a little muddy. Usually you will know if you have the type of rapport to ask to meet your person's peers. If you don't think you will get permission, don't ask.

You personally cannot risk going around your contact, regardless of the relationship, without their blessing. Any strategies will use other people within your organization without your knowledge. Within your company you have a full range of people to use to achieve the goal of parallel positioning. Again, if you have a marketing idea that will benefit your customer's marketing group, take yourself out of the loop and brief your marketing person and have them contact their counterpart in the other company directly. If you want your executive to begin a rapport with their CEO, then have him or her call that person directly. It very well may come back to your contact that these events have occurred. You will be shocked to hear about it, as you had no idea, and then you inform your client that you will find out exactly what is going on. If your associates have done their work of offering a compelling reason to establish a relationship, it is too late for your contact to halt any progress anyway. Depending on the level of bitterness, you may want to stay out of those other areas of activity to maintain the relationship. Your explanation is that, unbeknownst to you, there were initiatives from completely separate organizations within your company. It won't happen again, you promise. Well, it won't happen again that particular way.

If your company and or customer host a golf event then make sure that you invite the key executives from your prospect or internal. Your contact cannot possibly blame you if his boss and yours hit it off at a golf event. If you don't have these formal events, then arrange an informal foursome and round out the four with two other influential people within the account. Fishing, baseball, football, et cetera—all work for these seemingly serendipitous meetings.

With every new contact that you meet follow up with a handwritten note. During the main holiday season there should be sent at minimum a season's greeting card. For the more important contacts at the C Level (CEO, CIO, COO, CFO, COB) holidays are an opportunity to introduce yourself through gifts like tasteful baskets that will not be forgotten. A hundred dollars spent on a large account is a minuscule investment that will offer significant returns.

4

Differentiate or Die

Victorious warriors win first and then go to war, while defeated warriors go to war first and then seek to win.
~Sun-tzu, The Art of War~

We are moving along in the process that will result in the appointment. We have territory, target companies, and have identified the decision makers. The next step is strategizing how to establish contact with these people and with what message.

To reach them, I recommend letters of introduction, as they are more professional, better received and yield greater returns than an unsolicited phone call. They take more time than just picking up the phone, but produce more appointments and more sales. Some of your competitors may use contact center agents to try and close business and appointments. The letter approach will completely differentiate you from these and the bulk of the competition.

The message is vital to your cause, because your average decision maker receives a minimum of ten calls a day from salespeople trying to sell them a myriad of products. A good sales pitch is ineffective if you consider the number of times the prospect has heard it. Do you react positively to a telemarketer calling you at home with the same tired script?

That is why it is so important for you to do something different than the competition. Your first step to stand out is to send a concise letter. Second, base your message upon your research, and the third step is to have a strategy that will clinch the appointment.

The *right* letter, with the *right* message to the *right* person will mean an appointment *right* now.

The message or hook—You need a message to hook their attention. There are always several strategies that you can use for each of your prospects. You can use the corporate message that comes down from the head of your organization. They have spent a large part of their time developing solutions to differentiate themselves in the industry. At the very least, you should carry their strategy of differentiation to your prospective and current customers. Following are additional strategies of differentiation that you can use in conjunction with your leader's market message.

Strategies of Differentiation

Increasing prospect's sales—An example of partnering is when I discovered that my largest prospect was trying to sell into my industry. I met their salesperson and COO over lunch to strategize on how to sell to my company as well as my competitors. As a result, the account sold a six million-dollar deal to my employer. This in turn resulted in the customer sending more business my way.

Co-marketing—In another example of being a partner, I was working with a customer who was designing an incentives program to give their customers frequent flier-type rewards. We arranged meetings with our own marketing department to develop a co-marketing plan for both companies to increase sales.

Improve customer service—A utility company anticipating a new competitive landscape approached one of my associates. They were seeking to hire and train people with better customer service skills in order to differentiate themselves from their competition. My associate arranged a meeting with our company's human resources department to exchange ideas.

Overcome challenges—Another prospect was challenged with finding good people. I arranged a meeting between them and our human resources department that resulted in a referral program from our nonhire list.

Education—Another company was considering expanding their business into outsourcing outbound calling, but needed education. They took a tour of our outbound call center, where they met the management and the representatives making the calls, and this let them experience the entire culture.

Open new markets—In my international sales role, I was often able to approach prospects with a unique offer. I would stand out from the competition by positioning my solution as a way to enter new markets with practically no expenditure.

The Macy's Santa Claus solution—There are many prospects that need solutions that your company can't adequately fulfill. If you have no real competitive offer, don't drive your product down their throat. Differentiate yourself from the competition by finding a cost-effective solution from another company and suggesting it.

Whatever your customers' goals are, be there with a value-added solution. Increase their efficiency. Improve their customer service. Shorten their delivery time. Increase their profits. Your product or creativity will fit something that they need and position you for the sale.

Reciprocity: playing hardball—We were pursuing a large ski resort company who would barely let us in the door. When they did, they would punish us by glad-handing us on every occasion. This account was where I learned the term glad-handing for the first time. No matter what we did, they would not give us a fair opportunity at the business. What was even more maddening about this situation was that my company was a large customer of theirs, and every year had recognition events at their site. We would bring this up, and the customer would acknowledge and consider it; and when we left our proposal, he'd grin, throw it out, and stay with our competition.

After a few years our company finally decided to create a program that would identify the companies that sold to us. They then sent that information to the field where we would pursue these accounts with the specific financial information we were spending. There was a ripple of excitement and surprise throughout the sales force as they saw on that list the names of those companies that had treated us with hostility and disrespect.

Suddenly, with a single phone call from our procurement people to the VP of the prospect's sales group, the situation would rapidly change.

There are a number of ways to approach this with your customer. Arrogance is not one of them. Nor do you want to come out and refer to this, as I have, as reciprocity. A better way to phrase this plan to your prospect is "a fair exchange of business."

Here is an example of how delicately this subject must be treated: we worked on a company that had given us more than a fair shot at the business. My director started playing very heavy-handed with the account, which to the customer became not selling, not partnering, not a request for a fair exchange of business, but extortion. The customer suffered through the threats, and the moment they didn't have to do business with us, they were gone for good. Play this card; play it well, but play it soft, or it will blow up in your face.

The way to approach this is to first have the buyers from your company calling their contacts and clearly stating the need for a fair exchange of business. If there are no clear results within days, then have that buyer call the prospect's executive level and repeat the message. That will get results. Make sure that the buyer has the name of the person that you have been either working with or pursuing. If that person has ruffled feathers as a result of this strategy, then explain to them over lunch or golf that it was a company-wide initiative over which you had no control.

Odds are that your company does not have this type of program set up, where you will just receive a list of current relationships. There are two ways to fill this vacuum. One is to make internal calls to the procurement, finance, or accounts-payable people within your own company. Ask them for a ledger by payee, preferably with the financial detail. They may be reluctant to give out the numbers, so be prepared to go without, at least initially. You will need those numbers to play your hand right. If you are only spending ten dollars a month with FedEx, it won't help your efforts with the account. Once you get this list you have a strong prospect base.

The other way goes back to research. Through Internet sites like Hoover's, company press releases, annual reports, 10-Ks, and more, you can and will find mention of the prospect's customers.

Amateur Alert

Please do not be one of those people prospecting from the Yellow Pages. They call the secretary and ask who makes decisions on whatever they are selling. Talk about falling on your sword. People who do this are calling companies they know nothing about, asking a minimum wage earner for critical advice, and then using that information as their strategy for selling. This is what the sales trainers that have never sold or bought tell you to do. This method is a quick path to burnout and career change.

In the previous chapter, I discussed the benefits of reading the annual report and finding out everything you can about the company and its top officers. What you need to look for are opinions and quotes from the executives about their goals, objectives, obstacles to overcome, and so on. Your challenge is to find ways that your service will help them in accomplishing their objectives and goals.

The annual report and prospectus will also describe facts about the company's operations, and will often quote other key officers. Take their words, mention them in a letter, and explain how your service can benefit them.

If you still cannot find this kind of information with all of the resources I have mentioned, stand back from the company you are pursuing and contemplate the industry-specific challenges. For example, as of this writing, telecommunications and personal computer companies are having a very difficult time increasing shareholder value. What can your service do to assist these industries?

Particular positions within a company have identifiable hurdles that you should focus on. Vice presidents of sales are always looking for ways to improve close ratios and reporting tools. Marketing people are always looking for creative ways to reach customers. Financial people seek ways to increase profitability. The company president seeks to increase earnings per share.

Think hard about what will make decision makers listen to you versus the other sales calls they will get that day. Find out what keeps them up at night, address it in a letter, and you will have an audience, a customer, and commissions.

PART II
Methods of Contact

Am I not destroying my enemies when I make friends of them?
~Abraham Lincoln~

5

Letter Writing

The most valuable of all talents is never using two words when one will do.
~Thomas Jefferson~

The purpose of this chapter is to discuss writing professional, targeted, tailored letters to individuals, _not_ bulk mailings. Letter writing is critical in fulfilling this book's goal of assisting you in working smart and increasing your close ratio.

By using this method, your success rate will be greatly enhanced, so spending more time on fewer accounts is warranted. Also, it is a waste of time to write and send a hundred letters and not have the time to follow up. It is difficult to estimate the correct number of letters to start with, as territories and responsibilities vary, so start small and adjust based upon your success level. If you are just starting a job and have a clean slate, then twenty letters per week is a good start. As the weeks pass and the numbers of prospects mount, scale down on new letters and focus on closing the appointments.

If you already have clients and are looking to build your base, then ten is a more manageable number. You also will have to consider the fact that you may have four letters to four different individuals in one company. The key is to ensure that the number is within your grasp for follow-up.

Therefore, if you want to make an impact on the person you are trying to reach, craft a letter that will do just that. Do *not* leave droning voice mail messages. You will lose them, or their secretary may screen it and delete it when they hear who you are. Differentiating means doing something different; therefore, write an excellent letter.

This is the definition of a good letter: brief, concise, grammatically perfect, and tailored to that one specific person.

This is the definition of an excellent letter: includes all of the above plus the mention of industry-specific information, organization-specific information, and quotes that came from either the recipient of the letter or someone within their organization, preferably their boss.

When writing a letter, realize that you have less than thirty seconds to keep the reader's attention. Every letter should be tailored to the individual needs of their industry, company, title, and person.

What should you say?

Your goal is to take your entire sales strategy and put it into several sentences that deliver a punch to the decision maker's stomach.

How should you format it?

First, your letter has to appear short so that while scanning the pile of mail on their desk, they see that your letter is not time-consuming and they can glance at it and be done with it. If it is unread, it is nothing. Make it concise, and it will be read.

Second, it needs to grab their attention. Begin with a quote from them or their boss. They will be hooked and impressed.

Third, the letter must have a benefit for them. One of those sales classes stuck—WIIFM—What's in it for me? Tell them why and how they will benefit. Now they will listen.

Fourth, a next step must be stated and it must be bold. Don't go through all this effort and be meek. The customer has a need, you can fulfill it, and they want to see you. Tell them you will call for a meeting.

Fifth, sign it.

Sixth, hand deliver it. Don't mail it.

Here is an example:

Dear Mr. CEO,

I have been following your company in the media and market for over two years. Recently I read an article in which you stated, "It was foolish to continue using the old technology because of its limitations, so we gave it up."

I also observed in your annual report that your cost of services is up 57.7% in 1997 and 71.6% in 1996.

My company has a network-based technology that will safeguard your company from obsolescence and reduce your cost of services, which will result in an increase in your earnings per share.

I will call you to arrange an appointment to discuss this capability.

Five sentences covered it all.

Another example was also to a CEO:

I was fortunate enough to attend your presentation at the Power Breakfast, and I came away inspired and renewed by your outlook and contribution to the community.

Prospect's international initiative could not come at a better time to take advantage of an increasingly competitive telecommunications landscape. The merger of Company 1 and Company 2 has resulted in decreased costs for our global customers.

My goal as the national account manager is to understand your goals and establish solutions to assist in their attainment. Your mention of reaching a rate of X cents per minute in Europe is a significant challenge that I have taken on, and I feel confident that this can be eventually attained through Company 1/Company 2, especially with the expert negotiators on hand at Prospect. Our current list pricing is in the mid-Y cents per minute, so given the proper volume and term, costs in the .X are not out of reach.

I will continue to work with Joe and Jim with this mission in mind and look forward to providing you with information that will encourage you that soon yet another of your goals will be accomplished.

Longer, but the end result was good. I mentioned his specific goals and quoted him.

Now here is a letter to the VP of investor relations.

In reading the 2000 Annual Report it is made clear that communication with your clients is one of your highest priorities. In Prospect's Bill of Rights it states, "Information should be communicated in an understandable fashion." Company 1 has the capability through a recent acquisition that will assist you in achieving that goal.

Company 1 recently purchased Company 2 Teleconferencing that was one of the world's largest conferencing companies and the author of the Investor Relations conferencing concept.

I will call to arrange a time for us to meet and discuss Company 1's different capabilities within the Investor Relations realm.

You will notice that the letters are brief and always have some type of information in regards to the target person's specific goals. *Their* goals, not yours. We all know what salespeople's goals are. We have three letters, two of which mention information gained in the annual report, one which is based upon a chamber meeting, and half of the information in another coming from the newspaper.

This goes back to the chapter on research; now it all ties together. On closure of the letter, many people will tell you to mention a specific date and time to reference the follow up. If your schedule is nonchaotic enough to pull this off, then it is highly effective. Do not miss the stated date and time, because that affects your credibility.

There is much discussion on the advantages of teaching visually versus via audio. What is read will be retained longer and will have more impact than a verbal message. There is no opportunity for the target of your letter to be surfing the

Internet while reading your letter. A written document is not easily deleted or saved to listen to at another time. Certainly it can be thrown out, but if the letter's message is short enough and good enough, it will be read and positive action will be the response.

Also, what are your chances of reaching the CEO or president directly without a letter of introduction to break the ice? It can be done, as I will show, but these royal persons of corporate America are very protected.

Usually, the screeners have read the letter and delivered it themselves, if they think it is worthy of such an honor. Your average administrator, who would not hesitate to hang up on you, still has respect for the U.S. mail, and very rarely feel so arrogant as to throw out mail that is not addressed to them.

Many of us read mail and correspondence during our daily commute or at home, but can the letter reader bring home voice mail messages or your verbal communiqué to dwell upon in a quiet moment? Even if the concepts that you have written of do not match with their strategy, then at least you have reached the executive offices with creative ideas that set you apart from the competition. Think about the impact of a letter signed with your name, expressing interest in helping the CEO reach his goals.

Does that set you apart?

Does that assist you when your contact goes to that level for approval on your contract?

Does your competition do this?

Does anyone do this?

Should you?

Yes.

Hell yes.

Hell no.

Not really.

Yup.

So, do you stick it in the mail and be done with it? No. Find a very professional cover binder that will stand out. If your company does not produce a clean looking deliverable, go to a stationary store and get an 8x11 folder that will look presentable to an executive officer. In this case, contain your flamboyance and avoid the pinks and pastels.

If you have supporting documentation to include with your letter, place it inside the package and paper clip your letter (not folded) to the outside of the cover so that they won't have to open anything to see how short and clean it is. This way it will catch their eye.

The documentation might be anything ranging from a highlighted annual report page to an article mentioning their competition's strategy.

Mail it now? It depends. If you are geographically challenged, mail it, but an overnight service will assist in making it stand out. If the account is worthwhile, deliver it with a basket of fruit or a good bottle of wine (if they don't frown on gifts). Stand out. Get their attention.

If you have a smaller territory, hand deliver the letters. The impact of your driving and hand delivering something that could have been thoughtlessly stuck in the mail will help your cause. It will also assist in establishing that all-important relationship with the front desk. Also, going back to the cold-calling chapter, you might even get to meet your target, or at least an assistant who might coach you on the best way to reach him. Even those accounts a couple of hours away are worth the trip if they are of considerable size. Make sure they realize where you drove from so your interest level is clear. And cold-call on the way there and back for new opportunities.

6

The Campaign of Terror

The history of the world is full of men who rose to leadership, by sheer force of self-confidence, bravery and tenacity.
~Mahatma Gandhi~

Now you will experience the beauty of your hard work. This is not a cold call, but a warm call that is based upon all of the research that has gone into your letter.

There are entire books that dwell on the subject of call reluctance and what a person will do to avoid picking up the phone and having to face the perceived chance of rejection. The previous five chapters have both assisted you in that effort and alleviated your need to make those calls. By creating and employing a thorough, effective pre-call strategy, we have delayed the call, but more importantly we have reduced the chances for rejection. Call reluctance has been served and denied. The actual fear of rejection should be eliminated; as with all things, great preparation results in attaining great confidence. You will now experience less resistance and significantly greater success.

The letter was dropped off to the individual yesterday, and now is the time to make the first call. At this early juncture, you are being a pest. This is okay, because one of two things has happened. Either they have read the letter and your call will reach them while the letter is fresh in their mind, or they have not read the letter and your call will make them look for it and draw their attention to your interest. It is better to be too early than too late. If you wait too long, you are being unresponsive and they will forget about you and toss the letter.

Your letter and relationship building will have smoothed the usual blockers over a little bit. Nonetheless, let's do our best to avoid the wall that surrounds our target.

Question one—Do you have the direct number of your contact?

If your research has not uncovered the Direct Inward Dial (DID) number to the executive, you will have to run the normal course of reaching the receptionist or automated attendant, and then the executive assistant, and then, finally, the executive. If you have the DID, you can call your target and possibly cut out the blockers. Often, they will screen the DID as well.

Question two—If no DID then when is the best time to reach him or her?

Your average executive is usually a very driven individual, putting hours in before the administrative people arrive and after they leave. The screeners punch a clock to start their day at 8:00 or 8:30 AM, go to lunch from 12:00 to 1:00, and leave at 5:00. Therefore, work those hours when they don't. You will either get your person or someone who will blind-transfer you in. The executive will be impressed with your work ethic of pre-eight and post-five. They will listen to you more attentively because they are more relaxed; their day has neither begun, nor is it over, and they are undistracted by the normal chaos of 8:00 AM to 5:00 PM. They will also admire a fellow go-getter, and may reward your behavior with an opportunity.

Question three—You are staring at the phone and breathing calmly, what now?

First, be in a comfortable setting. Do you mind people listening in? If you don't mind, get set at your office and move to the next step.

If you do mind, as many do, find a conference room or uninhabited office and close the door for privacy. If you can, call from home.

Second, set a time limit for your calling. Know that you will call from 7:30 AM nonstop until 10:00 AM. This gives you a time goal and a light at the end of the tunnel for a much-needed break. Burnout is quickly achieved by making calls from 7:00 AM to 6:00 PM Break it up with appointments, lunch meetings with vendors, and dropping off your letters. Don't do it all at once.

Third, set an appointment goal. You will call until you get four appointments or you won't stop calling. Don't try each company one time per day. If you keep getting voice mails, don't leave a message. Call every hour until you reach them live. It is better to try this repetition on a direct number so the receptionist is unaware of your efforts. They will recognize your voice if you keep calling.

If it is a woman you are trying to reach, and you are a male, and you leave her a voice mail every hour, you might find yourself answering some tough questions from the authorities. Don't make them angry by filling their voice mailbox.

Fourth, have the letter you sent them in front of you so you can reference it in your conversation. Go over in your head what you want to use from the letter and what you don't. Highlight the key points in your letter, so you don't get distracted. Do *not* try to go over your solution over the phone. If they ask to discuss it, say it would be much easier in person, as you have to show illustrations and will have to bring an additional resource along. The goal is to close an appointment, not explain the solution. Chances greatly increase when you meet with them and establish a relationship. You cannot build rapport over the phone, you can only destroy it.

Fifth, *always* anticipate reaching your person. I was trying to reach one guy forever and never could. I called him regularly for months, and whenever his name popped up on my computer program, I routinely dialed anticipating his voice mail greeting and hanging up.

One day he actually answered. I stammered through the worst sales pitch I ever made. He told me he was not interested and I had no comeback, none. I never reached him again. Of course, the sales guy next to me was listening in, and just shook his head in disgust.

Sixth, anticipate objections, write them out, and have them memorized. The result of this approach is to minimize objections up front in order to facilitate the close of the appointment. However, you will still face the occasional diluted objection, so be prepared.

Seventh, have your calendar open with dates so you can close quickly. Before each call, have a good understanding of which times and dates you are available. Do not get into a chess match on coordinating your schedule. Do not appear disorganized before you even see them. Take whatever date you can and get off the phone. If it conflicts with internal meetings, take the customer appointment first.

Eighth, remember your goal: the appointment. Don't focus on anything else: not on rapport, on the weather, not on selling outside of what it takes to get the appointment. Executives have little time for socializing with their own family, let alone insincere solicitors. Agree on the time and get off of the phone.

Ninth, keep track of the order you are calling these accounts. Don't build a spreadsheet, but have some organization so that you know you have called ABC company before eight, and during lunch, so next time try after five. I will discuss software in a later chapter, but for now make sure you have a program that will organize your order of calling. If you do not have access to a computer, then go the tickler-file route.

Tenth, get your attitude straight: have a positive mental attitude. You will have some bad calls, but be glad that you got them out of the way, because you are that much closer to the great opportunities. On occasion you might get hung up on. Who cares? Be happy that you are not that person and do not have to talk to salespeople all day for minimum wage.

Eleventh, inspirational quotes and pictures can have a huge impact. Create a positive surrounding with pictures of the people or pets that you love on the wall, stories of people who overcame significant challenges in front of you, and personal goal phrases taped to the phone or computer. It may be difficult to pick up the phone again after a hang-up or a particularly nasty person. Visual reminders of your purpose will get you over these distractions fast.

Twelfth, practice what you will say out loud. Not ten times, but just once or twice to see if it feels comfortable coming out of your mouth.

Thirteenth, smile

Fourteenth, dial for dollars. Create your future now.

Question four—You have them on the phone—now what?

Follow your program as discussed in point four above, and close hard for the appointment. Again, have dates and times ready, go through your message, and close by asking would next Tuesday or Thursday work at 10:00? Get them looking at their calendar, not working on an objection. Control the call. Close, set the appointment, thank them, and hang up.

Question five—You get their voice mail, should you leave a message?

No. You don't know yet how they use their voice mail. They may use it for screening calls, like many people in Corporate America. Their phones are always forwarded and they return calls to whomever they choose. Don't leave multiple messages before you have an initial conversation, because you are giving them ample warning that you are hunting them. This causes them to mentally build up rejections for when you do speak.

For the initial contact, try to reach them as described above. No voicemails equals no warnings.

Question six—You still get their voice mail and it has been three days since you dropped off the letter, what now?

It is time to leave a very short, professional message echoing the contents of your letter.

Good morning Ms. Big, my name is August Specht and I am calling to follow up on a letter I dropped off on Monday. As I referenced in my letter, we have been able to find solutions to the same challenges you referred to in your 2000 annual report for XYZ Corporation and I would like to share that information with you, preferably early next week. Please call me at 555-8181. Thank you.

This way they know that you are following up as committed to in your letter. That message was only twenty seconds.

Question seven—It has been a week and they have not returned my call, what now?

Don't panic. They may be out of town, they may be buried with normal business, they may be interested but have no time to call or discuss. Your solution is still valid. They also expect you to follow up; after all, they are the customer, and you the salesperson. Enjoy the hunt, now is the time for real fun. Call them back, and if you continue to reach their voice mail, after a few attempts try one of my favorite tactics, the *drop by:*

"Mr. Hunt, August Specht again in reference to my letter on cost cutting ideas. I understand you are busy. I will be meeting XX company right next door on the sixth and will drop by to see you, shake a hand and drop off a business card around 2:00. If that is okay, I will see you then, no call back required. If not, give me a call to reschedule at 555-8181. I look forward to meeting you."

This works well. Every once in a great while someone doesn't approve of this technique, but it is less than one percent. If they aren't available for the appointment, you can still leave your card, some golf balls, a follow-up letter or information package, and gain some advice from the receptionist or the contact's administrator and then follow up with them. Make it sound like you had a firm appointment, express your sorrow for missing them, and state that you would like to reschedule with some potential times. Now, they feel like they owe you for not being meeting with you the first time.

Question eight—Okay, I have followed all of these steps and still had no luck. What's next?

I am a firm believer that the people who call the most, win the most. Therefore, make the decision of when to continue and when to move on to the next step and the next chapter, "Maintenance."

While deciding how to move forward with this contact, consider the following statistics:

80% of all sales are made after the fifth call.
48% of salespeople call once and then quit.
25% call twice and give up.
12% make three calls and stop.
10% KEEP ON CALLING.
THIS 10% MAKE 80% OF THE SALES.

My recommendation is therefore: *keep calling.* It won't kill you to invest thirty seconds or less several times a week to keep an eye on these accounts and to catch them in a different state of mind. You cannot just call an account once, get blown off, and then not call back. Selling begins when the customer says no. If the customer is adamant, stay professional and change your strategy to maintenance, which will be explained in the next chapter.

These steps and the following chapters work. The most important attributes of a salesperson are tenacity and differentiation. Use both in every aspect of your career and you will go far.

In closing, it is important for you to demonstrate tenacity and to wear down your target via multiple callings. But this is best performed after an initial conversation that leads either to rejection or to follow-up items. It is unprofessional to call over and over again without a good business reason. If you get denied, stand back, look at your strategy, and pick out step two.

On occasion, accept the fact that your contact hates you and/or your company. Move that person into maintenance and go after another title in the same company. Remember to have a strategy that encompasses more than one person to call at any one account. If you work several at once, you will get into the account. Just make sure your success comes at the executive level and do not get stuck with a low-level person, which will strictly gain you a false sense of accomplishment.

7

Dialing for Dollars

As is our confidence, so is our capacity.
~William Hazlitt~

Before I was forced by a controlling sales manager to go knock on doors, I was exclusively a phone zealot. I would make over a hundred calls on many days, typically either qualifying leads or following up on a qualified lead to make the appointment.

Now after almost twenty years in sales, I primarily believe in knocking on doors as part of research to prepare a letter, and then a phone call for the close. I could sell exclusively by the phone under the belief that I was saving time, but I have learned that face-to-face prospecting increases my appointment close ratio, defeating the argument of saving time.

I have done both styles of prospecting. Regardless of your particular preferences, strengths, and industry, don't get too caught up with the efficiencies of e-mail, voicemail, text messaging, and so on. People buy from people, not voices over the phone. Your decision maker's screeners will let you by more often if they have met you in person before you call.

For those of you who still prefer to work the phone instead, or as part of a strategy, let's move forward. Given that you are not covering pavement, then your world becomes reliant on the quality of the data that you are using to call from. I have used many different types of lists, ranging from Dodge Reports to the Yellow Pages to the *American Business Journal's* Book of Lists, and they almost always have two things in common. One, they typically aren't inexpensive, and two, they are always overworked by salespeople. If you do invest in these lists, you will either face a very hostile contact who feels harassed and overwhelmed by the number of calls from salespeople from numerous industries, and/or you will be able to bid, but your competition will be numerous, fierce, and a decision will be based upon low bids.

Therefore, instead of chasing your tail by spending a great deal of money on these lists, I recommend that you leverage the efficiencies of the phone and blanket every square inch of your territory that fits in your target demographic. You will be in more deals, with less competition, and create a tickler file that will allow you to establish relationships with contacts that you will be regularly speaking to until they are ready to buy something. Beginning the relationship in advance will position you for the win, instead of working the lists and getting in at the last minute for the low bid.

Is your territory a ZIP code, city, skyscraper, or a vertical market in multiple states? All of these categories can be dissected either online or in print. Hoover's Online and the book *Contacts Influential*, or others like it, will provide you varying degrees of demographics based upon your preferences like geography, vertical market, special industry code (SIC), and/or size of the organizations. You can also customize within your territory to find key contacts based specifically on their backgrounds. I recently did a Hoover's search in a certain state for executives with the key word search *University of Florida*, which is my alma mater. I then had a list of executive prospects with whom I had a level of commonality to help break the ice. Resources like this are often free at your local public library or through a separate agreement reached by your employer.

Once you have that list, you need to prepare a method to qualify it. This method has to be customized to your specific solution. For example, if you are selling any solution that is oriented around relocations, then you would structure that into your qualifying statement. Moving companies, office supply firms, printers, telecom equipment providers, builders, and many others will be seeking those organizations making a move. If you have a service that fits a particular demographic, like small employers with ten to twenty employees, then you need to identify those accounts through your qualifying process.

The qualifying over the phone ultimately depends on two key things: you, and the receptionist who answers the telephone. Receptionists are often trained to not give out names, titles, or direct numbers. Aside from this, they are generally open to someone to talk to, as they are often bored or lonely. Therefore, in your qualifying, seek to disarm them when you get them on the phone. For example, tell them that you have to send an invitation to a seminar to their company's CFO, and that the dates and times are different depending upon what type of service they were currently using. Ask for their guidance help figure out the correct date and time. Then you start with your qualifying questions. Typically, you should use only a few critical questions that will tell you how to categorize the account.

It is important to limit the number of qualifying questions, so that the quality of the answers will not deteriorate and threaten your fledgling relationship.

The key facts to have as part of your qualifying process are typically number of employees, number of locations, type of company, industry, and whatever is customary to your industry. If it looks like the account is a viable prospect for you, ask for the name of the appropriate title you need. Don't waste your time trying to wheedle the person's name from the screener if the account is not within your target demographic.

In speaking to the receptionist, be very specific in the terminology you use. When I was first selling long distance services, many of us would repeatedly make a critical error when qualifying accounts by asking, "Do you spend a lot on long distance?" Almost always the answer was, "Oh yes. A ton of money." Talk about a lack of communication! When I would say "a lot," a thousand dollars or more a month is what I was thinking. The people on the other side of the phone were often thinking $100. Other examples are, "Do you have many employees?" and "Do you make a lot of phone calls?" I can't tell you how many times I would make an appointment with these "very large" accounts over the phone, only to go out there and see three cars in the parking lot, wasting their time and mine.

Qualifying accounts over the phone is very challenging, so you have to be creative in your techniques. The Internet is of course a huge asset in finding the right accounts for your services. You may be able to search their Web site and press releases to gain good information that will give you an impression of whether they are the right account for you. If you happen to know one of the decision maker's names, you can search for them online at www.Google.com, Hoover's, or a myriad of other sites. You will be amazed at what you can find out about them, as they may be in a calculus club, quoted as endorsing your competitor's products, or explaining why they went through a divorce.

Another idea is illustrated by what I had to do when I worked the phones in a several-county area in northern New Jersey. I was selling PBXs and key systems, and in telephone sales back then you were primarily replacing older Ma Bell equipment. Your qualifying process was to determine the age of the prospect's phone system. Of course, as a rookie I started out with another dumb question, "Is your phone system old?" The receptionist knew the extreme example of brand new versus antique, but that did not help me most of the time. After a while, I realized that the receptionists could read me the model number on their phone; that would tell me how old, how large, who sold it, and most importantly, if this was a short-, mid-, or long-term prospect. A Dimension phone system was an immediate hot prospect, while a Merlin was most likely a three-year wait for a sale.

Pick your qualifying questionnaire, orient it to the most critical information you need with several questions, try it for a while, refine it based upon your luck, and then work through your list and create a list of qualified accounts that you put into a software program like ACT! Even if the accounts do not fit your current profile, put them in anyway with a bare amount of information so you create a holistic view of your territory that you can use for many years in different positions.

On the accounts that do match your profile, take copious notes and put them into your tickler file. Include everyone you speak to and get many details on them like their age, children, and so on. The receptionists often hold the keys to the kingdom. It is important to rate them in a field in your database so you can categorize them by urgency level. You have to create a legend that you will understand. For example, hot, hotter, hottest might mean a month for a decision or follow-up, two weeks, and one week. Then sort by those categories to ensure that you work the best leads first, then the next level, and so on.

Here are some pointers on the statement itself. First, if you want to get hung up on all of the time, ask for the *decision maker.* This is a really bad idea: experienced receptionists dump amateur salespeople when they ask this question. Remember, this is qualifying; your goal on this call is to determine if the account is worth the many phone attempts you will make to get an appointment. This is not the time to get an appointment. Remember that activity does not equal accomplishment. Sales equal accomplishment, and if you consistently spend time on accounts that are not within your sweet spot, you will fail and get fired.

The statement I used when selling phone systems was very basic. I did need to know the size of the accounts to know if my phone system would have a chance of selling. My sweet spot was 20–80 employees for this particular product. Any larger or smaller and we lost all of the time, so I focused in on this segment. Again, I had to disarm the person on the phone, so I would not ask for the decision maker or the office manager.

My qualifying statement to the receptionist was, "We are having a seminar next month and we need to send invitations to the appropriate person within your company. I just have a couple of questions to determine which seminar they should attend." The questions I then asked were the following:

- Would you happen to know what type of phone system your company uses?

- How long have you had it?

- Are you relocating, expanding, or opening new offices?

- Thank you. We need to send the invitation to your chief financial officer. How do you spell her or his name?

Get off the phone, write down you notes, including the receptionist's name, rank it in level of urgency, and move on to the next call.

You should be able to create your own qualifying statement now. The next step is for you to organize a calling schedule based upon your peak times for performance. Charisma is vital in working the phones, as the timbre of your voice is all that you have working for you. White teeth great hair, and Italian suits make no difference over the phone. Your charm, your tone, and your delivery are going to make the difference. Pick your peak time of day to make these calls. If, like many of us, come 2:00 in the afternoon you are hitting a point in the day when you want to put your head on the desk, don't make calls then. Pick your peak performance time and make the calls then. I am a morning guy with tons of energy and caffeine, so I typically try and organize my key customer-facing activities at that point in time to put my best face forward. Late afternoon, I'm a different person, particularly in the winter. If I have to call all day, then I'll orient my appointment-making calls for my peak times and drudge through the qualifying when I am subpar. No matter what, the calls must be made.

Before you make the appointment calls, you need to do a little more research on the names that you have gleaned in your qualifying process. Go quickly to www.Google.com and enter the person's name with quotes on either side, and see how many hits you get. If you get hundreds, then add the company name outside the quotes and that should narrow it down. Also go to the company Web site and see if there are biographies online. You will often get a picture and great background. Don't skip the Google search though, as you can get much better candid information on them that you may be able to reference in your appointment request.

Once you have called and qualified some leads that match your selling criteria, it is time to call for an appointment. Follow the same advice mentioned earlier in the book. I'll list the advice for you one more time:

1. Be in a comfortable setting where you don't mind people listening in, or where they can't listen in.

2. If at all possible, find a place with no background noise. This will build your credibility and not make it sound like you are in a call center.

3. Have your calendar open with several key times that you want to meet.

4. Have your appointment pitch ready.

Let's develop your appointment pitch. Have your best effort first, as you only have a few seconds to get around rejection. First, do not ask closed questions that yield a yes or no answer. Do not open with, "How are you?" or, "Do you have a moment?" You do not care how they are and they know it, and whether or not they have a moment, you are going to ignore what they say and ask for an appointment anyway.

1. Dial the number.

2. Introduce yourself.
   "Good morning Edward, my name is August Specht..."

3. Use a credibility builder as an add-on to your name, referencing your experience in their industry. Drop a competitor's name that you have worked with.
   "...And I have experience in working on solutions with Cigna and Aetna..."
   You have their attention—everyone wants to know what their competition is doing.

4. State a benefit that worked for their competition that will also work for them. Also reference any of your research on the person you are calling here.
   "...Your competition experienced a net increase of margins of over 1 percent as a result of our solution, and I note from your biography that your stated goal is to increase your company's margins..."

5. Ask them to select a time on their calendar between a couple of choices.
   "...I will be near your office next week on Tuesday and Thursday, which day would be best for me to stop by and introduce myself?"
   Sure, it is a sales call, but do not threaten them with blunt facts. You are just stopping by to introduce yourself, which will lead to a much longer conversation about your solution.

6. Get the time on their calendar; if they ask how much time, go for thirty minutes, with the goal to make your conversation so compelling that you make it go long.

Get off the phone. Do not provide contact details so they can cancel once they have remorse.

Here is my call sample:

Good morning, Mr. McGuire. My name is August Specht, and I am calling you relative to a solution that increased productivity and reduced healthcare costs at Cigna and Aetna. I have read in your annual report that increasing productivity and reducing healthcare costs are your main goals.

I will be near your office on Tuesday and Friday of next week, and can drop by to introduce myself if you have a few minutes.

Tuesday at 2:00? See you then.

Thank you.

Spend some time in research that will tell you their goals, and you will increase your appointment-setting close ratio.

Some key points for success include the following:

- Be polite and professional

- Be concise

- Be sincere

- Show you know their business

- Illustrate you know their goals

- Provide a couple of options for a short meeting

- Get off the phone

<u>Objections</u>

There are many potential objections, and you have several general techniques to overcome them.

- Attempt to anticipate everyone and practice overcoming their objections. For example: I do not have time to meet you. Some possible responses are:

  - "I completely understand how busy you must be with your efficiency initiatives; would you like to meet during breakfast or lunch?"

- "Well, who else is involved in this project that could afford fifteen minutes out of their schedule to hear how we benefited your competitor?"

- If you cannot overcome the objection, then acknowledge it and use the "stop by" technique.

- If neither of the above tactics works, then use the "wear-down," or "campaign of terror."

The "drop by" has worked for me for many years. The way it works is that after they reject you, you respectfully accept it, then tell them that as you will be in their building or next door the following week, you will just stop by and drop off a card so they have your contact details. They will typically say sure and get you off of the phone. Put the time you referenced down and make good on your word and "stop by." When you go to the reception desk, ask for them as if you have an appointment and they will typically come out and at minimum shake your hand. Human nature is to be less aggressive in person than over the phone, and they will most likely open up to you. Take advantage of the face-to-face and triage a 30-second pitch to convince them to spend more time with you. It may also be a good idea to bring a small gift like golf balls, a pen, or something else along those lines.

If the "stop by" fails, then the next chapter, titled "Maintenance," will work for you.

8

Maintenance

Always bear in mind that your own resolution to succeed is more important than any other one thing.
~Abraham Lincoln~

Your appointments will be the result of a combination of strategies. Many will come through catching the right person, at the right time, with the right solution. Some will come by the continued calling and wearing down of their resistance. Yet others will come as a result of pure persistence and tenacity over a period of time. This latter strategy is the subject of this chapter.

You reached the account and discussed your ideas with your prospect. They told you that they are not interested at this time, to call back at another time, or the dreaded, "Please send me information." Regardless of what they said, they have not given you an appointment at this time. Therefore, you need to implement a strategy with these people. You need to develop a maintenance plan that will keep your name positively in front of your prospects for consultation. The goal is to establish value so that you will be the preferred vendor when contract time inevitably arrives.

Maintenance will be deployed in a number of measures based upon the account. Some people may not be opposed to seeing you, but cannot buy at this time due to any number of reasons, such as budget, contract, and so on. Other people may have absolutely no intention or desire to ever see you or do business with you. Both of these types of clients require a regular strategy that will not allow them to forget or dismiss you. Your objective is to wear them down through positive methods that assist them with their goals, but will not immediately benefit you.

We all have quotas, and you cannot spend time making friends with people that can't do business with you. But skip some personal lunches, time on coffee, and cigarette breaks, and you will find the time to meet with these people. Short-term selling is a result of having effective long-term selling strategies.

First of all, you need to understand what will help your account in a different way than we did to get the appointment. Remember, if you are working with the IT group, then the CIO lives in daily fear that the CEO will ask him about a technology that he has never heard of. This same type of fear applies to all departments across an organization. Become their resource and educate them on industry trends that may benefit their business.

How? Read, read, read. Gather information on the trends in IT or in your customer's industry. For example, I knew that one of my customers was interested in entering fulfillment, and I had just read an associated article on that subject. I made a copy, put it in a package with a note, and dropped it off.

It may not apply, but they will be impressed that you thought of them. When it is decision time, they will remember those little things you do that your competition doesn't.

The best method to accomplish this goal is to establish a monthly news package tailored to each prospect, without making it a major undertaking. If you are selling to primarily financial types, orient your newsletter to that group in a mass-production, generic fashion. This will save you time and energy. Introduce the package with a polite letter without the sales pitch, and outline the information within the package. They will be surprised that it is not the standard material that a marketing department puts out.

The newsletter will consist of the following items:

1. A cover letter that explains the contents, but no sales pitch explaining why your company is the best ever. This cover letter is a form letter created with a program like ACT!

2. A professional folder for the contents

3. The contents

    a. Your customer's industry developments—for example, an article about the customer's competitor who implemented a new cost-cutting strategy

    b. Your industry developments—for example, updated information on Y2K was a very popular topic of conversation in the telecommunications industry

    c. Clippings from articles that pertain to your customer's business or trends—for example, if a customer has a sales force working from home, include articles on the pros and cons of telecommuting.

Another example: the customer is anticipating relocating, and you see an article discussing how to select a mover.

Sign the cover letter and send the package. This is maintenance, so you do not need to drop it off, unless you want to stop by and see who you might bump into.

The news package is not the full extent of your efforts. I have worked with other salespeople who actually design a full-blown newsletter using desktop publishing. They create the newsletters based upon a combination of clippings and their own writings. They mail these out monthly to a large group of prospects that can use this objective information to their advantage.

Depending on your customer and your technology, you should have a more immediate "news flash" type of information that you can send to your customer if the timing is more important. A good example is that you read about an IPO that should be a good stock pick, and you know that your customer is a big investor. Send an e-mail or a fax giving them the heads up. Both fax broadcasts and e-mail broadcasts deliver flash information.

The goal is to stay in front of them. It demonstrates your follow-up and tenacity before the sale, and they will reward you with an appointment and with business.

PART III
Strategies to Improve

We know what we are, but know not what we may be.
~William Shakespeare~

9

Tenacity
&
Caller Reluctance

Nothing in the world can take the place of persistence. Talent will not; nothing is more common than unsuccessful men with talent. Genius will not; unrewarded genius is almost a proverb. Education will not; the world is full of educated derelicts. Persistence and determination alone are omnipotent.
~Calvin Coolidge~

My initial training with MCI in December of 1990 had, aside from the usual stuff, a session on caller reluctance. Caller reluctance is a subconscious behavior, indicated by stalls created to delay having to pick up the telephone and make a call to a potential client. This is a natural aversion to an unpleasant task, which is what some people consider making a sales call to be.

What are some symptoms of caller reluctance?

- Spending too much time drawing up lists of people to call instead of calling them

- Over-researching territories

- Doing e-mail

- Cold-calling and over-qualifying instead of actually making the call for an appointment

- Meeting with your network so that you feel like you are accomplishing something

- Making excuses for not calling that day: stock is down, bad timing, raining, bad mood, Monday blues, Friday stress

- Insisting on complete privacy to call; this is a preference, not a requirement

These are just a few of the symptoms, and it will not be hard for you to identify them once you start doing it. It is no different from school when you went to the library with a friend, and as soon as you opened your books, you had a million things to talk about. When you know about it you can defeat it. Identify the problem and eliminate it by focusing on your goals and all of the worthwhile accomplishments you are striving for. Then pick up the phone and dial.

I tied tenacity into this chapter because overcoming caller reluctance requires tenacity. You must have the ability to keep going on against negativity and rejection. As will be discussed in the Goals chapter, you have to make goals to pull you out of the morass and to stay focused. I am a big believer in quotes, because they tell you what other people have accomplished in much more difficult situations than you and I will probably ever face, and for considerably less reward.

Customers will reward your tenacity. Secretly, they admire people who keep pursuing them and don't give up. Many times I have seen them shake their head with a smile as they describe a particularly tenacious salesperson who just won't give up. So don't.

There is no failure except in no longer trying. There is no defeat except from within, no really insurmountable barrier save our own inherent weakness of purpose.
~ Kin Hubbard ~

10

Goal Setting

It's not enough to be busy. The question is: What are we busy about?
~Henry David Thoreau~

After graduating from the University of Florida, I had $81.00 in the bank. I returned to my parent's home in New Jersey, where I had to save money and look for a job. My first sales job and territory was in Newark.

It was not an easy transition going from living in Florida to being thrown into grim Newark. In order to survive this absolute hell, I set a goal of getting back to Florida the first chance I could. When I had interviewed with my new employer, I noticed the map of their locations illustrating several in the Sunshine State. I decided to join the company with the intent of transferring intra-company back to Florida ASAP.

However, I knew that this would not be accomplished by a mere phone call to human resources. To accomplish this goal, my numbers had to be high enough to create interest in those Florida offices. My sales would only result by staying focused through the days of rejection and frustration. To stay focused, I set reminders of my goal to return to Florida.

I wrote out the word Florida in tropical colors and taped it to my phone. Whenever I thought I could not stand another minute of hang-ups and rude people, I looked at that Post-It note and refocused on my goal. In twelve months, I climbed from number 110 to number four in my company and strolled into my next assignment in Tampa, Florida with a full relocation package.

Years later, I was having a real crisis with sales and feeling crummy about the whole profession. Reflection and introspection caused me to reconsider my path and concentrate on the past instead of the future. This self-doubt came at a strange time, because I was making incredible money and had blown out all of my goals. What occurred to me then was that I needed new goals in order to stay focused. I wrote down all of the things that I wanted to do, including a laundry list of places to visit and retirement objectives. I considered whether or not I could accomplish these goals with my current income and career path, and realized that they were all attainable.

Remembering my former Florida Post-It note and needing visual reminders to stay focused, I drew up another note on which I wrote, "Sales is the Vehicle." I wrote this specifically due to my being burnt out with the entire idea of day-in, day-out selling long distance dial tone. I had to remind myself that I was working not to sell long distance, but to make enough money to retire early, travel, and achieve financial freedom. These were my goals, and it did not matter if I shoveled horse manure, cleaned septic tanks, or swept streets, as long as those actions propelled me towards my long- and short-term goals.

These days, goal setting is all the rage, which it should be, and many have heard the saying, *"It is a dream until you write it down, then it becomes a goal."* Write down your goals. Have short-, mid-, and long-term goals. Years ago when I would sit through endless meetings, I would multitask by dividing my attention between the speaker and my jottings of all the goals I sought to achieve.

I still have these planning notes that show a vertical flowchart of activities that I built from the bottom up. At the bottom of this particular goal-setting exercise was the mid-term career goal of having an international travel position. It would allow me to live in a foreign country and see the world. From the goal at the bottom, I built in all of the options and steps back to where I currently was to achieve my goal.

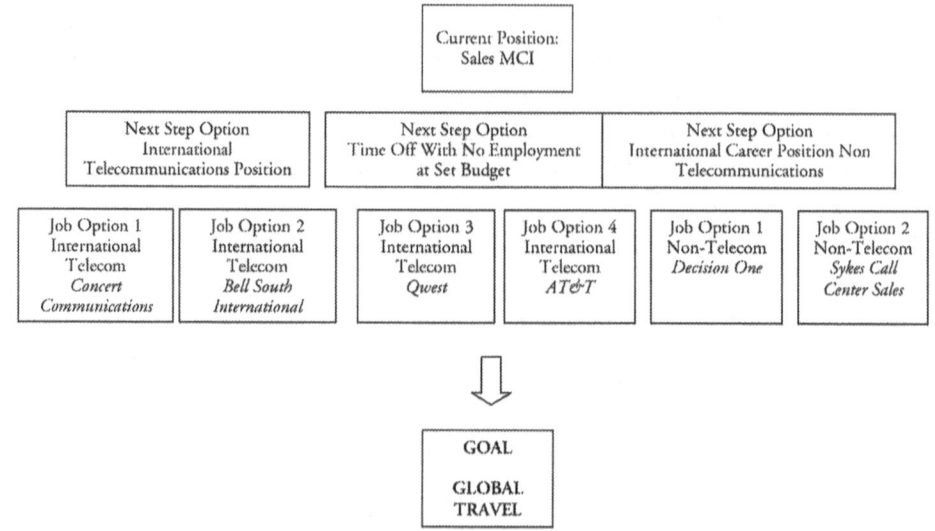

Following the flowchart, I began to further establish relationships within each of these options to position myself for opportunities.

What was the result of this planning? As I write this chapter, I am traveling on a train through Italy with my lovely wife. All of my written goals and dreams have led me to this place with this wonderful woman. Dreams can come true if you recognize them and if you give them life by changing them into goals.

"Chance favors the prepared mind."

What does this quote mean?

If you know that you have a goal of going overseas, and you have an acquaintance mention that he has heard of a job overseas, it clicks. How many of these passing opportunities do we miss every day because we are not focused on a goal?

I firmly believe that without a written goal, you are a ship without a rudder. Not only are you missing opportunities that you should be taking advantage of, but you are likely to run smack into depression. We all know people who have failed at something simple like a diet, but are successful at all other endeavors. Why? They failed to set personal goals for their weight program. By not setting goals, we fail to plan, which means that we plan to fail.

Do you want to start running to get in shape? Then set a goal. Find a short run six months into the future. Set the goal to run it and finish at a certain time or place in a certain range. Work backwards from that goal and plan what you need to do to accomplish it. For example, run three miles at a pace of nine minutes per mile. Know that you need to run X times a week, and Y miles per run. You know that you must incrementally increase your pace by Z to get your pace from 9 minutes per mile to 8.5 minutes per mile. With a set, written goal, this can be accomplished and you can do it.

A famous example of the power of written goals is Lou Holtz. When I am goal setting, I always think of his story. At the age of twenty-nine, with his third child on the way, he found himself unemployed, broke, and dispirited. His wife gave him a book called *The Magic of Thinking Big* by David Schwartz. To help people like Holtz get motivated, the book recommended that they write down all of the goals they wanted to achieve before dying. Holtz followed the advice to the letter and wrote down a list of 107 goals.

The list, when written in 1966, seemed impossible, as it included appearing on *The Tonight Show with Johnny Carson*, seeing the pope, winning a national championship, being Coach of the Year, landing on an aircraft carrier, shooting a hole in one, and having dinner at the White House. He used the list as a guide and a measuring stick of his success.

This list changed his life and allowed him to reach goals that many of us would never even dream of. My research has showed that he has attained eighty-one of his goals, with twenty-six to go.

11

Crash Course to Success

The reason a lot of people do not recognize opportunity is because it usually goes around wearing overalls looking like hard work.
~Thomas A. Edison~

Who will win and who will lose in the sales game? What if your competitor is your mirror image, who reads the same things you do, has an equally great product, has the same charisma, and has the same positioning with the customer? Who wins? The answer is not the one with the lowest price. It is the one who works the hardest.

On CNN recently, a CEO was asked what was the secret to his success. His answer, albeit simplistic, is good advice: "Work Saturdays, because your competition doesn't." He is right. Differentiate yourself from your competition by making a personal commitment to bury them with activity.

Be everywhere. Have your competitors asking the famous quote from the movie *Butch Cassidy and the Sundance Kid,* "Who are those guys?" Be those guys.

One time I was working on a small deal that practically every competitor in our industry was trying to win. I had an appointment there, and while I was waiting, the receptionist told me to wait longer as the controller was in with Sprint and the president was talking to Cable & Wireless. There were three competitors in the same building at the same time.

I won the deal by showing more interest. I would stop by regularly, sometimes without notice, just to drop off information that I purposefully did not have at an earlier engagement. I used these relationship-building techniques to outposition my opponents. They were waiting by the phone for the decision, while I was smalltalking and closing the deal.

Look at Steven Spielberg. Behind his talent and ability is also a work ethic that many of us cannot match. He made an agreement with his wife that he would work all hours for a year, then take two years off and work normal hours and spend the proper time with his family. He used his own version of the Crash

Course to Success. Of course he was already incredibly successful, but the strategy worked for him. In one year, he produced three of the best movies ever made, and earned an Oscar as well as a ton of cash. He then returned to a more sane life with his family.

Another example comes from the biography of John Grisham. He demonstrated incredible focus and discipline in writing his first novel, *A Time to Kill*. Every day for three years, Grisham wrote from four to seven AM. Then he would go through his normal day of making a living like the rest of us. It paid off.

Crash Course is not a program that you do for your entire life. You can, but I disagree with the mentality of sacrificing everything for your job. If you debate this, take the FranklinCovey course "Seven Habits of Highly Successful People." That will get your priorities back in line.

So, what is the Crash Course to Success? It is a program that I developed very early in my career, and it is very simple. For a set period of time, I recommend six months, you will do the following:

During business hours, from 8:00 AM to 5:00 PM, you will only talk to prospects. That's it!

What does this mean? Between 8:00 AM and 5:00 PM, you will *only perform customer-facing activities*. There is only one exception: you do still have to attend meetings with your boss and participate in training classes. Any other activities under your control can only happen after five or before eight.

Here are the activities listed categorically:

Between 8:00 AM and 5:00 PM (includes lunch)—key selling time—you can complete the following activities:

- Cold-call customers

- Telemarket customers

- Go to appointments with customers

- Meet with vendors to discuss customers

After 5:00 PM or before 8:00 AM, or even Saturdays, you can complete these activities:

- Meet with internal resources

- Meet with management (it will get you a raise from a good boss)

- Complete expense reports

- Create presentations
- Develop proposals
- Write letters
- Read industry information
- Conduct product research
- Conduct prospect research
- Conduct executive research
- Conduct territory research
- Complete internal reports
- Fill out sales orders
- Fill out service orders
- Catch up on e-mail
- Write or create newsletters

This is an easy concept, but a difficult task. Here are some techniques to make it easier:

E-mail

If you establish this plan and your intent is to work late rather than early, do not turn on your computer until after 5:00 PM. E-mail is a trap that will suck you into other people's initiatives instead of your own. If it is truly an urgent issue, fellow employees will escalate to your voicemail, which should have the same message that your e-mail does, "I will be on appointments all day but will check messages and return calls at my first opportunity." Do this *after* 5:00.

Work from Home

The social and political temptations of the office are a magnet for distraction. There are plenty of unsuccessful people who believe that their careers and their place of employment are extensions of their goal of pursuing and maintaining social standing.

On a daily, and often hourly basis, I would have people come by my desk and have conversations with my back. Always my back, because if I turned around and engaged them, I would be lost for hours. I made it my mission never to be that great, popular guy that was fired. I knew people who wanted to be popular above all other priorities. They reached their goal at every one of their jobs that they were last fired from. Sales is not the place for office popularity contests. Be popular with your family, your customers, your accountant and your sales manager. Work at home.

Train Coworkers and Boss

Explain to your coworkers, manager, sales support, and receptionist that you are coordinating your activities within your Crash Course strategy. They will not only support you, but also admire you, and the smart ones will emulate you.

Most importantly, do as Steven Spielberg: *gain acceptance from your family.* Tell them that your plan is only for a set time, and that this will give you enough momentum to carry you for years. If you do not get buy-in from your family, *do not do it.* It is not worth risking your marriage, relationship, and your children's upbringing. The rest of this book still applies, it will just take longer for you to ramp up to the high level of activity.

When I first implemented this program, I remember describing the result to a colleague. "I have been pushing this snowball up a hill for months and it has grown bigger and bigger, and heavier and heavier. I finally reached the top. Now gigantic, it is chasing me back down the hill. I am running as fast as I can, just trying to stay ahead of it."

This story represented the very high amount of activity I had generated through Crash Course. It created a four-year run of nonstop success for me, and for years after it benefited those who inherited my base of accounts.

Genius is one percent inspiration and 99 percent perspiration.
~ Thomas A. Edison ~

12

Technology Tips

Veni, vidi, vici.
[I came, I saw, I conquered]
~ Julius Caesar~

If you are not PC literate, take a night or weekend class now. Otherwise, you will not be able to compete effectively against people who benefit from technology. Every decision made in sales should be made in consideration of outpositioning the competition. Therefore, you must always have an edge on them. Your advantage can come through reading books like this, working harder, working smarter, and, for the purpose of this chapter, using every minute more efficiently by adopting technology early.

This chapter is not only about the Internet and personal computers, but all types of technology available today. Some of this will be obvious, some new, and some outdated by printing time, but the theme of this chapter is to seek technology to assist your efforts.

I no longer have to work the kind of hours I used to for a number of reasons. One reason is that I am more efficient than my competition, because I am an early adopter of technological trends. Many of us quota bearers have windshield time (traveling), and one of the ways to get home before 10:00 every night is to use every minute to its maximum. Technology allows us to be super-efficient. Instead of losing two hours in commuting and then having to work late to catch up, run up the cellular phone bill and be productive.

Technology will get you home on time, and with your job done. No technology is cheap, but if your company does not reimburse you, ask them to. If they still don't and you want to stay working there, purchase the technology anyway, and you will have a good return on investment. As of this writing, if your company won't reimburse you it is a tax write-off.

The Internet

I entered the business world in 1988, and had to wait six years for the Internet. The difference between the way I used to do research on prospects and the way I research them now is like night and day.

The wonders of the Internet provide salespeople today with incredible intelligence on their accounts, prospects, and executives that in the past was difficult to find. I am tempted to belabor the point, as it is imperative to adapt to this trend in order to survive. Don't fight it, embrace it, and you will not only compete at an even level but you will also keep your company ahead of the others around the world that are slow to catch on. The Internet is as American as apple pie, so support it and work more effectively.

It is vital to your pursuit of information that you get online and use a few of the following Web pages for your research.

With the millions of sites on the Internet as well as the hundreds of publications about the Internet, you will have to periodically read the "best of the Internet." These are my tried-and-true favorites.

Web Pages

Hoover's Web page: http://www.hoovers.com

You can gain a lot of free information on your accounts from Hoover's. For a small fee that is well worth it, you can find an incredible amount of information on financials, executive backgrounds, and so forth.

Competitors of Hoover's that offer similar capabilities are:

www.marketguide.com

www.corporateinformation.com

All three sites offer a great search capability that can be defined by company name or other parameters. You may have determined that your product sells well in a particular niche like airlines. If so, you can find that industry type either through a classification term or a standard industry code (SIC) and search on these sites for other companies in that industry. You can define your search through geography by ZIP code, state, and/or area code.

Gale Biographies: http://www.galenet.com

This is an excellent site that provides detailed information on executives.

AltaVista: http://www.altavista.com

I have been using different search engines for years, and AltaVista seems to bring up more defined answers than most of the others. With all search engines, you place the company name in the search box, press enter, and you will get very good information about most companies, whether public or private.

All portals: http://www.yahoo.com, http://www.aol.com and many others allow you to create a personal site customized for your purposes. I use Yahoo to track my investments as well as to keep an eye on top prospects in the news.

CompanySleuth (http://www.companysleuth.com) is a tool that e-mails you regular updates on companies that you select.

Local newspaper Web pages: They are on the web and they have search capabilities in their archives, so you can get all of the information on companies and executives.

American City Business Journals: http://www.bizjournals.com

Most major metropolitan areas have some sort of business journal at this site. Go to this site and subscribe to this excellent publication. It also you to search archives for anything business-related in your geography.

They also publish a *Book of Lists*, which is a great reference tool that ranks the top businesses in a number of ways. These companies are the most prospected, but are very viable for pursuit.

Financial Times: http://www.FT.com.

This is an excellent site for general research on companies, industry, trends, and so on.

Annual Report Library: http://www.prars.com

This site allows you to order customers' annual reports.

Two-Way Pagers

One-way pagers are not much more than an annoyance. If you are in a meeting, you cannot just jump up and leave to call, unless you get the infamous 911. Two-way pagers are more expensive but are worth every penny, because they allow you to reply back to people who page you without completely interrupting a meeting or conference call.

I was at a client meeting receiving pages on negotiating from my boss, who was at the other end of the table. Coverage right now is not great outside major metropolitan areas, but for urban warriors they work great. I highly recommend them.

Cellular Phones

If you don't have one, get one.

I had a friend who complained that his cell phone never allowed him peace during the day. I countered that if you used it enough during the day, then you would have peace at night. It shortens your day and keeps you ahead of the other guys by being more responsive to your customers. It also allows you to utilize every minute of the day efficiently. The old days of windshield time where you lose hours driving are gone. Sales calls and follow-up can happen every minute of the day with a cell phone.

Laptops versus PCs

PCs restrict your efficiency, and laptops increase it. Buy a laptop every time. Sales careers have several paths and almost always involve travel and relocation. It is very frustrating sitting on a plane, on a train, or in a terminal for a few hours thinking of all the things you could do if you had a laptop.

When you do get a laptop, buy the key accessories such as extra batteries, back-up drive, extra power cable, and telephone cables. If you travel overseas, get international adapters for power and telephone lines. If you are buying the laptop, get the extended warranty.

Back up your information on a backup drive on a regular basis and invest heavily in an anti-virus capability.

Also, you have the ability to connect to the Internet and receive your e-mail via wireless capability. This could be crucial if you are traveling and need to pull your e-mail. Having wireless access frees you from hotel rooms and all of the traps associated with the local telephone companies, international phone companies, hotel billing, dialing sequence strings, and so on. Of course, it would only work from moving vehicles as long as the wireless company does their part. This is especially beneficial if you travel overseas. The speeds are slower than U.S. standards but still functional.

Activity Software

ACT! is my preferred customer tracking software. Earlier, I discussed tickler files and that is what ACT! is, plus a complete word processing capability and more.

Handheld Organizers

Palmtops or handheld organizers have been around for a few years now, and I recently purchased one. If you are a road warrior who likes to travel light, this is for you. This technology replaces your need for a paper-based organizer or, at minimum, complements it. Some come with wireless Internet access, making this the ultimate tool for salespeople.

13

To Do or Not to Do

They are able because they think they are able.
~ Virgil ~

Do—Find out if any executives in your list of prospects went to colleges where you or people in your office did, and coincidentally meet them at an alumnus gathering.

Don't—Go over the head of a contact with whom you are already working. This does not work and will backfire every time. Instead use a partner, associate, or manager to contact another individual within the company. If it fails and comes back to you, it won't be the same as you doing it, and you can pass it off as coincidental or unrelated to yourself.

Do—Find out if any companies in your territory sell services to your company. Approach your purchasing or procurement department, get a list of companies, and pursue them in a big way. This will greatly increase your close ratio and make for some quick, easy sales. If they don't play ball, escalate to procurement and have them contact people within your target company to apply pressure.

Don't—Buy the phone blow off, "Please mail me information." This is a typical way to get you off the phone, not an interest on your prospect's part. Regroup and use another strategy, including a different contact to pursue.

Do—Only work on accounts that are headquartered where you can establish a face-to-face relationship. Customers buy from people they know and like. You cannot do this on the phone.

Don't—Use the Yellow Pages for cold-calling. You have no information on anything specific to that company, and you will fail.

Do—Go out and mix at community events, as you will bump elbows with your prospects and have occasion to establish relationships and a network.

Don't—Do mass mailings to prospects. Customers recognize them for the generic items that they are, and ignore and trash them. The one to three percent returns that you get are not worth the time spent.

Do—Present your solutions to user groups. There are many councils and organizations that meet on a regular basis.

Don't—Fail to differentiate by dressing down like the current trend. Your customer deserves and expects your respect. If you are the only one not in a suit competing for that prospect you may lose.

Do—Ignore my previous statement if the customer bonds better with people that dress like him or her. Make your appearance contact-specific, and when in doubt, overdress.

Don't—Forget to ask for referrals from customers that you have sold to. This is a post-sale technique that will net you a fast appointment and sale.

Do—Be careful with your overall impression. If you absolutely have to buy that Porsche, Mercedes, or Ferrari, get in the head of your buyer. Will this specific individual be impressed, or turned off? I have had prospects negatively comment on my competition driving Mercedes, with a clear reference to their prices being too high. If you need to, borrow a Honda for your hyper-perceptive prospects.

Don't—Pay any attention to No Soliciting signs. You aren't selling anything that minute. You are only gathering information for invitations to an event. Really. The people that hide behind these signs are often the easiest to work with. The sign is their only defense and they know it.

Do—Avoid having security throw you out by prospecting an office tower from the top down. Walk into the building like you work there, head straight for the elevator, and go to the top. Lobby lingering will result in your being asked to leave by insecure security.

Don't—Ask for the person you are calling in an overly formal manner. Always use a first or nickname to get past the screener. Bill instead of William, but probably Richard rather than Dick.

Do—Use other forms of differentiation in the sales process in order to win. Be more responsive, more knowledgeable, more polished, more ethical, more personable, more charismatic, more interested, more enthusiastic, and more reliable, and you will win more often.

Don't—Fail to buy this book for friends, family, associates, strangers, and passers-by.

Conclusion

You can do anything if you have enthusiasm. Enthusiasm is the yeast that makes your
hope rise to the stars.
Enthusiasm is the sparkle in your eyes,
It is the swing in your gait,
The grip of your hand
The irresistible surge of your will and your energy to execute your ideas.
Enthusiasts are fighters,
they have fortitude,
they have staying qualities.
Enthusiasm is at the bottom of all progress.
With it there is accomplishment,
Without it there are only alibis.
~ Guido Scano ~

Now that you have completed this book, you are ready to close appointments. The tools in this book will also enable you to achieve your own life goals and objectives.

However, there is another area that you will need to continue to research. The subject: you. It is not sufficient to become an expert in any subject area, unless you deliver that knowledge with spirit and passion. In anything that we try to accomplish, we will find our success or failure lies in our degree of enthusiasm.

Early on in my sales career, I was very fortunate to work with an incredible group of salespeople, two of whom were Bill Wohlrob and Neil Kaiser. Bill, Neil and I worked on many deals together. I remember an occasion when a prospective customer remarked how Bill and I seemed so different from our competitors. Bill, being not only a consummate salesperson but also, and more importantly, a thoroughly honest man, replied that it was because we liked what we did and it showed.

He was right. Out of that crummy little smoke-filled, rundown sales office, we closed a ton of business in the year before I transferred to Florida. I assure you that we had at best a fair product, lousy sales support, pretty good pricing, no name recognition, and zero corporate direction, but we won almost all of the time. We were successful due to our energy, attitude, experience, optimism, enthusiasm, and team play, in spite of the company we worked for.

You have to embrace, grasp, hold the ideas in this book and take them to your task with hope and optimism. This is an attitude that will carry you far in any venture you pursue. When you get that occasional hang-up in your ear, smile and think, "I'm glad I got that out of the way." Then go on to the next call. The next one may very well be what you have been striving for. Look at rejection, not as what the word implies, but as part of the process of reaching success.

I have included quotes from incredible people throughout this book as messages of hope and wisdom.

If you are unsure of your ability, and your confidence is lacking, understand that it's merely your perception of yourself instead of a reality.

Read self-help books. I highly recommend *Success Through A Positive Mental Attitude* by Napoleon Hill. It will point you to many more attitude-boosting works by great leaders. Self-esteem, integrity, self-discipline, and attitude are critical criteria to success and are completely within your control.

Now, go get them!

APPENDIX A

Other Resources

American Firms Operating in Foreign Countries
> This text is an excellent tool if you are pursuing companies that do business outside of the United States. Unfortunately, at this time it is only available in text, so you will either have to purchase it from the Department of Commerce or find it at your local library in the reference section.

State World Trade Centers
> Many states have set up World Trade Centers to assist them in attracting foreign investment and to facilitate local businesses in conducting business overseas.

Some states have International Directories that can be found through these organizations: http://world.iserve.wtca.org/

Cole Directory

Contacts Influential

Standard and Poor's Register of Corporations, Directors and Executives.
> Key executives in 32,000 leading companies, plus 75,000 directors.

Who's Who in Finance and Industry

American Business Directory

Chamber of Commerce Directories
> Usually only accessible if you join the Chamber or go to the local library.

The Almanac of American Employers 1996–97.
> Focuses on the 500 largest, fastest-growing, most successful corporate employers; covers companies of 2,500+ employees.

Plunkett Research, Ltd., P.O. Drawer 8270 Galveston, TX 77553. 409-765-8530.

Corporate and Industry Research Reports.
Published by R.R. Bowker/Martindale-Hubbell, 121 Chanlon Rd., New Providence, NJ 07974.

Corporate Jobs Outlook!
A newsletter published every 60 days, available in most public libraries. This publication covers companies of 500 to 2,500 employees. Many jobs sources are excellent references for finding good prospects that are experiencing rapid growth.
Plunkett Research, Ltd., P.O. Drawer 8270, Galveston, TX 77553. 409-765-8530.

Corporate Technology Directory.
Lists companies by the products they make or the technologies they use. Corporate Technology In-formation Services, Inc., 12 Alfred St., Suite 200, Woburn, MA 01801-9998.

Dun & Bradstreet's Million Dollar Directory

Dun & Bradstreet's Reference Book of Corporate Managements.

F & S Index of Corporations and Industries.
Lists published articles by industry and company.

Fitch Corporation Manuals.

Fortune Magazine's 500
One of a genre that also lists Forbes, Inc. and many others.

Macmillan's Directory of Leading Private Companies.

Standard and Poor's Corporation Records

Standard and Poor's Industrial Index.

The Adams Jobs Almanac
Has a state-by-state index of the major employers. The same publisher has an excellent JobBank Series that you can find in your local bookstore or

library. Currently there are JobBank books for: Atlanta, Boston, the Carolinas, Chicago, Dallas-Fort Worth, Denver, Detroit, Florida, Houston, Los Angeles, Minneapolis/St. Paul, New York, Ohio, Philadelphia, Phoenix, St. Louis, San Francisco, Seattle, Tennessee, and Washington DC. There is also a National JobBank. By the Editors of Adams Media. Adams Media, 260 Center St., Holbrook, MA 02343.

Hoover's "The List of Lists"
HTTP://www.hoovers.com/company/lists_best/0,2561,141,00.html.
It connects to all of the major company listings such as *Fortunes, The Standard, Forbes, Top 100 Web Sites,* and *FT Times Most Respected Companies.* This is an incredible free Internet site.

Thomas' Register. Thomas Publishing Co.
There are 27 volumes in the Thomas Register. All the manufacturers there are of 52,000 products and services, plus catalogs, contacts, and phone numbers.

Walker's Manual of Western Corporations.
Walker Western Research Co., 1452 Tilia Ave., San Mateo, CA 94402

APPENDIX B
Motivational Material

Obstacles are necessary for success because in selling, as in all careers of importance, victory comes only after many struggles and countless defeats. Yet each struggle, each defeat, sharpens your skills and strengths, your courage and your endurance, your ability and your confidence, and thus each obstacle is a comrade-in-arms forcing you to become better...or quit. Each rebuff is an opportunity to move forward; turn away from them, avoid them, and you throw away your future.
~Og Mandino

We are what we read. These books will inspire you and change your life, like they have for me and millions of others. This listing is just the tip of the iceberg. Read them, believe them, and incorporate their lessons into your life. You will be amazed at what you can achieve.

Books:

Dig Your Well Before You're Thirsty: The Only Networking Book You'll Ever Need
    by Harvey Mackay

Unlimited Power: The New Science of Personal Achievement
    by Anthony Robbins

Swim with the Sharks without Being Eaten Alive: Outsell, Outmanage, Outmotivate, and Outnegotiate Your Competition
    by Harvey Mackay, Kenneth H. Blanchard

Beware the Naked Man Who Offers You His Shirt: Do What You Love, Love What You Do and Deliver More Than You Promise
    by Harvey Mackay

Think and Grow Rich
    by Napoleon Hill, Melvin Powers

Success Through a Positive Mental Attitude
    by Napoleon Hill

Seven Habits of Highly Effective People
    by Steven R. Covey

Living the Seven Habits: Stories of Courage and Inspiration
    by Stephen R. Covey

Over the Top
    by Zig Ziglar

A Better Way to Live
    by Og Mandino

The Greatest Salesman in the World
    by Og Mandino

The Holy Bible

Biographies:

Thomas Jefferson
George Washington
Benjamin Franklin
Michelangelo
John Adams (by David McCullough)

Quotes:

If we did all the things that we are capable of doing, we would literally astound ourselves.
—Thomas A. Edison

The family you come from isn't as important as the family you're going to have.
—Ring Lardner

Resolve to perform what you ought; perform without fail what you resolve.
—Benjamin Franklin

The quality of a person's life is in direct proportion to their commitment to excellence, regardless of their chosen field of endeavor.
—Vince Lombardi

Anyone who has never made a mistake has never tried anything new.
—Albert Einstein

The meek will never inherit marketshare.
—Bill McGowan, founder, MCI

If A equals success, then the formula is A equals X plus Y plus Z. X is work. Y is play. Z is keep your mouth shut.
—Albert Einstein, recalled on his death, April 18, 1955

Everything comes to him who hustles while he waits.
—Thomas Edison

Failure is only the opportunity to begin again more intelligently.
—Henry Ford

Whether you think you can or think you can't—you are right.
—Henry Ford

There is a real magic in enthusiasm. It spells the difference between mediocrity and accomplishment.
—Norman Vincent Peale

Believe you are defeated, believe it long enough, and it is likely to become a fact.
—Norman Vincent Peale

Plan your work for today and every day, then work your plan.
—Norman Vincent Peale

Your enthusiasm will be infectious, stimulating and attractive to others. They will love you for it. They will go for you and with you.
—Norman Vincent Peale

Become a possibilitarian. No matter how dark things seem to be or actually are, raise your sights and see possibilities—always see them, for they're always there.
—Norman Vincent Peale

We tend to get what we expect.
—Norman Vincent Peale

The best executive is the one who has sense enough to pick good men to do what he wants done, and self-restraint enough to keep from meddling with them while they do it.
—Teddy Roosevelt

In any moment of decision the best thing you can do is the right thing, the next best thing is the wrong thing, and the worst thing you can do is nothing.
—Teddy Roosevelt

Get action. Seize the moment. Man was never intended to become an oyster.
—Teddy Roosevelt

Associate yourself with men of good quality if you esteem your own reputation, for 'tis better to be alone than in bad company.
—George Washington

Be more concerned with your character than with your reputation. Your character is what you really are while your reputation is merely what others think you are.
—John Wooden

Not failure, but low aim, is crime.
—James Russell Lowell

Do the right thing.
—Tom Fletcher

What would life be if we had no courage to attempt anything?
—Vincent van Gogh

Ah, but a man's reach should exceed his grasp, Or what's a heaven for?
—Robert Browning

I like the dreams of the future better than the history of the past.
—Thomas Jefferson

The only place where success comes before work is in the dictionary.
—Vince Lombardi

For anything worth having one must pay the price; and the price is always work, patience, love, self-sacrifice—no paper currency, no promises to pay, but the gold of real service.
—John Burroughs

None but a mule denies his family.
—Anon.

I don't know who my grandfather was; I am much more concerned to know what his grandson will be.
—Abraham Lincoln

It's not whether you get knocked down, it's whether you get up.
—Vince Lombardi

You are the Sum Total of all the Decisions You make in your Life.
—Neil Kaiser

Courage is resistance to fear, mastery of fear—not absence of fear.
—Mark Twain

Far better it is to dare mighty things, to win glorious triumphs, even though checkered by failure, than to take rank with those poor spirits who neither enjoy much nor suffer much, because they live in the grey twilight that knows not victory nor defeat.
—Theodore Roosevelt

True courage is like a kite; a contrary wind raises it higher.
—John Petit-Senn

There has never yet been a man in our history who led a life of ease whose name is worth remembering.
—Theodore Roosevelt

It is hard to fail, but it is worse never to have tried to succeed.
—Theodore Roosevelt

Never leave that till tomorrow which you can do today.
—Benjamin Franklin

Things may come to those who wait, but only the things left by those who hustle.
—Abraham Lincoln

Putting off an easy thing makes it hard, and putting off a hard one makes it impossible.
—George H. Lonmer

Even if you're on the right track, you'll get run over if you just sit there.
—Will Rogers

In delay there lies no plenty.
—William Shakespeare

Procrastination is the art of keeping up with yesterday.
—Don Marquis

Always bear in mind that your own resolution to succeed is more important than any other one thing.
—Abraham Lincoln

The secret of success is constancy to purpose.
—Benjamin Disraeli

I know the price of success: dedication, hard work and an unremitting devotion to the things you want to see happen.
—Frank Lloyd Wright

It is not because things are difficult that we do not dare; it is because we do not dare that things are difficult.
—Seneca

If I had 8 hours to chop down a tree, I'd spend 6 sharpening my ax.
—Abraham Lincoln

Failed in Business in '31
Defeated for the Legislature in '32
Again failed in Business in '34
Sweetheart died in '35

Had a nervous breakdown in '36
Defeated in election in '38
Defeated for Congress in '43
Defeated for Congress in '46
Defeated for Congress in '48
Defeated for Senate in '55
Defeated for Vice-President in '56
Defeated for Senate in '58
Elected President in '60
~This man was Abraham Lincoln~

978-0-595-34957-9
0-595-34957-9